SIGHTINGS

SIGHTINGS

Extraordinary Encounters with Ordinary Birds

SAM KEEN

Illustrations by MARY WOODIN

CHRONICLE BOOKS
SAN FRANCISCO

LIBRARY OF CONGRESS CATALOGING-IN-PUBLICATION DATA AVAILABLE.

ISBN-10: 0-8118-5976-2
ISBN-13: 978-0-8118-5976-9

MANUFACTURED IN CHINA.

DESIGNED BY SUSANNE WEIHL | FOLIO2

DISTRIBUTED IN CANADA BY RAINCOAST BOOKS
9050 SHAUGHNESSY STREET
VANCOUVER, BRITISH COLUMBIA V6P 6E5

10 9 8 7 6 5 4 3 2 1

CHRONICLE BOOKS LLC
680 SECOND STREET
SAN FRANCISCO, CALIFORNIA 94107

WWW.CHRONICLEBOOKS.COM

DEDICATION

FOR PATRICIA DE JONG

*Arise up, my love, my fair one, and come away. For,
lo, the winter is past, the rain is over and gone. The
flowers appear on the earth; the time of the singing
of birds is come, and the voice of the turtledove is
heard in our land.*

—SONG OF SOLOMON 2:10–12

CONTENTS

White Heron

What lifts the heron leaning on the air
I praise without a name. A crouch, a flare,
a long stroke through the cumulus of trees,
a shaped thought at the sky—then gone. O rare!
Saint Francis, being happiest on his knees,
would have cried Father! Cry anything you please.

But praise. By any name or none. But praise
the white original burst that lights
the heron on his two soft kissing kites.
When saints praise heaven lit by doves and rays,
I sit by pond scums till the air recites
Its heron back. And doubt all else. But praise.

—JOHN CIARDI

INTRODUCTION

It is private life that holds
out the mirror to infinity.

—E. M. FORSTER

ONCE UPON AN IMPROBABLE TIME, in an unlikely city not given to adoration, an unexpected epiphany occurred. Shortly before Christmas, the only poor but contented residents of a Fifth Avenue cooperative were unceremoniously evicted from their home. The co-op board ordered its minions to destroy the nest of a pair of Red-tailed Hawks that had occupied a small ledge-sited penthouse for more than a decade. The hawks' eating and hygiene habits were simply unacceptable to the rich and famous. Too many pigeon feathers and inedible portions of mouse were falling to the sidewalks of New York.

Overnight, the cult of Pale Male and Lola came into being. Hundreds of citizens who were inured to crime and

grime flocked into Central Park with binoculars and telescopes, hoping to catch a glimpse of the blessed birds. The
scene was reminiscent of the appearances of the Virgin Mary
on remote Greek islands, which attract hordes of the faithful.
Web sites sprang up, chronicling every move of the couple as
they terrorized pigeons and devoured mice and rats. The
devout kept watch night and day and reported every return,
every gesture of affection, every twig carried in hope to the
site of the destroyed nest.

A widespread protest of the sacrilege went up from
the supposedly secular core of the Big Apple. Suddenly, the
honor and soul of the city were at stake. Could New York
allow such injustice to go unopposed? Could the modest poor
be displaced by the heartless rich? Could the last remnants of
the creatures of the wild be banished from the city? The
answer came loud and clear: no! The arrogant board failed to
understand that it had an obligation to be guardian of the
public, communal, and civic space, and that Pale Male and
his family belonged to all the people. Avian activists stood
out in the cold with pickets until the embattled apartment
dwellers were forced to rescind their decision and restore the
ledge to the homeless hawks.

With millions of eyes watching their every move, Pale
Male and Lola rebuilt their nest and prepared to start over
again. When nesting time arrived, anxious devotees kept
watch to see if Lola would lay eggs and produce fledglings.
The first eggs did not hatch. Many feared that post-traumatic

stress disorder had rendered the couple sterile. But in the fullness of time, more eggs were laid, chicks emerged from the shells, and fledglings took to the air. Across the city, the mood of mourning gave way to jubilation.

In their short time in the spotlight, Pale Male and Lola were celebrated on film and in print. Messages arrived on their Web site from around the world: "He is a good dad. The one we always wanted. . . ." "It restores my faith in nature. . . . My spirits are high; I know there is good left in the world." "You have brought wild hawks into my life and made me think of them and worry about them as a family. . . ."

Through the ordinary magic of the imagination, the two Red-tailed Hawks were transformed into winged messengers of the sacred. The gift they brought that Christmas season was the revelation that, beneath its profane facade, the prosaic city still believed in the poetic wisdom of Emily Dickinson:

> *Hope is the thing with feathers*
> *That perches in the soul,*
> *And sings the tune—without the words,*
> *And never stops at all.*

Judaism, Christianity, and Islam all claim a definitive knowledge of the nature, will, and purpose of God that was revealed to Moses, Jesus, or Mohammed, recorded in scripture, and mediated through cult, clergy, and creed. What the great monotheistic religions neglect to honor are the unique ways in which the experience of the holy comes to individuals. Being focused on the transcendent God, they tend to overlook the sacred moments—the sightings and peak experiences—when a solitary self stands in awe before the miracle of existence, is astonished by the grace of soaring Red-tailed Hawks, is moved by the beauty of a trumpeting stargazer lily, or is comforted by a sonorous symphony of frogs on a summer night.

Each person has a unique way of experiencing the world that reflects the multitude of events that make one person's autobiography different from another's. Our most intimate revelations of the sacred come in odd ways that may seem meaningless or trivial to an outsider. In those pivotal moments when we are struck dumb by the simple existence of a flowering tree, we detect faint echoes of an unknowable G—. A brief opening appears in the cloud of ultimate ignorance under which we dwell. Yet, the experience is so private, so idiosyncratic, that we don't know how to talk about it. We stutter in an effort to put into words something that is ineffable. But there is no way we can explain concisely why our self and our world are unaccountably changed by such encounters. The philosopher Ludwig Wittgenstein once said of this paradox of mystical experience: "There are things that cannot be put into words. They make themselves manifest. They are what is mystical."

But what is indescribable is not necessarily inexpressible. What cannot be said straight can be told on a slant. The experience of the sacred may be sung, chanted, danced, put into a poem, or embedded in a personal narrative, autobiography, or story. We may point to ways, places, and times in which we glimpsed the Infinite in some finite disguise. Poets have caught a fleeting glance of Eternity in a grain of sand or in a "Tiger! tiger! burning bright, / In the forest of the night." Norman Maclean's family found in fly-fishing the enacted metaphor of grace and love. Suffering from frostbite, Willi Unsoeld, a leader of the first American expedition to summit Mount Everest, experienced an opening to Eternity when he saw a blue flower coming out of a snowbank as he was being carried down the mountain. For the philosopher Ernest Becker, as for so many parents, it was the birth of a child: "I think the birth of my first child, more than anything else, was the miracle that woke me up to the idea of God, seeing something pop in from the void and seeing how magnificent it was, unexpected, and how much beyond our powers and our ken." The history of religion can be seen as a catalog of the ways the Formless One has been experienced in the Sacred Many. It has appeared as a holy man or woman—shaman, prophet, healer, avatar, bodhisattva—or as a snake, bear, cow, pig, horse, river, or spring. So a Red-tailed Hawk may become a living metaphor of the Divine.

Each of us constructs a worldview and philosophy of life in which certain persons, places, things, or events take on an extraordinary burden of meaning, assume a revelatory significance in the dramatic narrative by which we make our lives understandable to ourselves and others. Perhaps at the precise moment at which I see a butterfly emerge from a cocoon, a switch is flipped, and what was, a second before, a purely biological event suddenly fills me with a conviction that all life is a miraculous transformation. Think of the slight adjustment the eye makes that reverses figure and ground in the classic gestalt puzzle, so that at one instant we see a goblet, and at the next, two faces turned toward each other. Suddenly, an "accidental" happening becomes a coded message that speaks directly to our condition.

Since all such moments happen to solitary humans, they are inevitably embedded in personal narratives, stories, and autobiographies. Only by sharing my stories can I give voice to those moments when my private life has been touched by Eternity, by the Unknown G—.

This brings me to the feathery messengers who have been my private angels.

When Job's friends presumed to understand the ways of God and the reasons for his suffering, Job, none too gently, advised them: "Ask the beasts, and they will teach you; the birds of the air, and they will tell you; or speak to the earth, and it will teach you; and the fish of the sea will declare to you. Who among you does not know that the hand of the Lord has done this? In his hand is the life of every living thing." (Job 12:7–10)

As I explore the numinous moments that have been central to my life, I often turn back to an enchanted time in childhood when I wandered freely in the woods. It was in those wild places that the love of birds and the quest for G— intertwined to fashion the double helix that has informed my journey.

I have not always been swept off my feet by the appearance of a Black-and-white Warbler or of a Bald Eagle. To paraphrase Freud, sometimes a bird is just a bird, not a metaphor. But the birds I am writing about here are those that have opened new vistas, inspired my mind to ask new questions, made my imagination soar, and caused my spirit to expand. The point of recording this journey is not to suggest that anyone buy a bird book and a pair of binoculars and take off for the wilderness, though that is never a bad idea. And if you are already a bird-watcher, you may have been blessed with similar insights. My experience is illustrative not normative. I offer this account of glimpses of the sacred that have occurred in my encounters with certain birds, snakes, and other creatures in the hope that it may be useful to others who are in quest of the places, experiences, and metaphors that undergird their sense of the sacred.

THE INDIGO BUNTING

FIRST SIGHTING

IN THE BEGINNING was the Indigo Bunting.

My love affair with birds began in the years before World War II. By the time I was ten, I had announced my intention to become an ornithologist; was reading daily from my personal bible, *Birds of America;* and was spending all my free time running wild in the woods.

Early on, I was satisfied to see the common species that inhabited the town and the woods—Red-headed Woodpeckers, robins, mockingbirds, Brown Thrashers, Yellow Warblers—but gradually I developed an inordinate desire to see something rare and exotic. A provocative description of the Indigo Bunting in *Birds of America* allowed me to focus my longing: "No other bird attracts quite the peculiar attention that this bird does. To get acquainted with him one must be prepared for surprises, and what they all are will not be told here. The male has such a peculiar color; no bird outside of the tropics has such a peculiar blue, a deep ultramarine blue. But you get the bird in a different light and behold he is gray-blue, or azure-blue or maybe olive-blue."

I had a strong premonition that my sighting of this marvel would signify something important, though I didn't know exactly what. No one in the fifth grade at Fort Craig Elementary School, where I was a painfully shy student, or at the First Presbyterian Church had ever seen an Indigo Bunting. They didn't even know buntings existed. If I could see one I might possess a secret amulet that would protect me from my persistent feeling of being a misfit. My love of birds, my worries about religion, and my habit of wondering about the ultimate whys and wherefores marked me as so different from the boys in the neighborhood that I often wondered if I was a sissy. Perhaps if the Indigo appeared, I would feel better about myself.

For months my quest yielded no results. I saw plenty of kingbirds and meadowlarks, but no Indigo Bunting. Then, when I least expected it—according to the note in the margin of my bird book—it happened. It was May 29, 1942, a hazy day so humid that the leaves shone with moisture. I was picking my way through the thick foliage en route to the creek, and although I was concentrating on avoiding the briars, I briefly looked up. There, perched on the top of a thicket, was the fabled ultramarine blue Indigo Bunting. And sure enough, in the interplay of light and shadow, he became lapis, cerulean, azure, olive-blue, and sometimes disappeared into the turquoise sky.

Time stopped. The woods evaporated and left me standing awestruck in the presence of the holy bunting. It was as if I was looking from the outside at a scene that contained only the bird and me. Effortlessly, I slipped into a state of grace in which I felt honored by a magical being that had previously only inhabited the mythical world of my *Birds of America*. At the same time, I was completely at ease and had a sense that the wilderness was my true home. I have no idea how long the sighting lasted because the Indigo preexisted in my imagination and perches there to this day in my memory.

What sent me forth on the quest for this particular bird? Why did the Indigo Bunting become my personal holy grail?

If I listen with "the third ear" to the description of the Indigo Bunting that I pored over so many times as a child, it is easy to uncover one reason for my fixation. "The male of the species is the most showy of birds, not afraid to exhibit himself on a fence rail." When other birds flee from the heat of the day, the Indigo "flies to the top of a telephone pole or the topmost twig of the tallest tree in the neighborhood and sings his roundelay of love." By contrast, the female is suspicious, secretive, silent, and sometimes as hard to see as a mouse in a thicket, a plain little brown-striped sparrow without a single distinctive feature. "Most observers see the male in the neighborhood and by a process of exclusion will decide the little brown bird is also an Indigo Bunting."

During my childhood, my father was frequently away from home, and I was surrounded by powerful women who fervently wanted me to share their religious visions and would have willingly designed my future. Not surprisingly, my longing became attached to a species of bird in which females remained in the background. When, I wondered, would I have the courage to sing my roundelay of love from the highest branch, to be as free as a bird?

I wanted to be the showy bunting who, like my colorful father (a choirmaster and virtuoso baritone), sang loudly and proudly. One day, my father, the master of the extravagant gesture, told me to pack a few clothes and get in the car. "Where are we going?" I asked. "It's a surprise," he replied. Two days and a thousand or more miles later, we arrived at Cornell University.

Without warning, we walked into the office of Dr. Arthur A. Allen, the world-famous founder of the university's ornithology laboratory, and my father announced that his son wanted to be an ornithologist. Dr. Allen listened, and then politely invited my father to have some coffee and cool his heels for an hour and said that he would give me a private tour of the rare-bird archives. Not entirely coincidentally, the most memorable moment of that hour was when Dr. Allen pulled the emerald green skin of a South American bird from a drawer. "Look what happens to this bird when it rains," he said, dampening his finger and rubbing it on the skin. Before my eyes the emerald feathers turned indigo. Once again, the bunting appeared mysteriously, out of nowhere.

But there was much more to my quest. At the precocious age of ten, I was already experiencing my first religious-spiritual identity crisis.

I was born into a cocoon of unquestioned faith, into a Scottish Presbyterian family in which Christianity was The Way, The Truth, and The Life. Right doctrine was a matter of eternal life or eternal death, so we believed the fundamentals: the verbal inspiration of the Bible, the virgin birth, the divinity of Christ, the substitutionary atonement, the resurrection of the body, the last judgment, and the second coming of Christ. We recited the Apostles' Creed without mental reservations, crossing our fingers, or demythologizing. No mushy Methodism or liberal modernism for us!

When I was eleven, I decided, not without subtle encouragement from mother and grandmother, to join the church. I can still see myself (like Jesus) standing before the elders, answering questions from the Westminster Shorter Catechism: "Q. What is the chief end of man? A. Man's chief end is to glorify God, and to enjoy Him forever. Q. What rule hath God given to direct us how we may glorify and enjoy Him? A. The Word of God, which is contained in the Scriptures of the Old and New Testaments, is the only rule to direct us how we may glorify and enjoy Him."

But as much as I tried to tailor my beliefs in God to win the approval of the adults who loved me, the form of Christianity that informed my childhood contained double binds, emotional and intellectual bear traps that ensnared my questioning mind and fervent heart.

My first ordeal, failure, and subsequent agony came about because I lacked any sense of having a personal relationship to Jesus. It was generally understood among the pious that right belief in the divinity of Christ was only the first baby step in becoming a Christian. Beyond that lay an intimate relationship with the Lord. Dutifully and with earnest resolve, I set out to find that relationship. Each afternoon I climbed into my tree house, pulled the rope ladder up after me, closed my eyes, and prayed to the impenetrable darkness that Jesus would enter my heart and take away my lingering doubts. Day after day I waited for the miracle to occur. It didn't. At long last, I was forced to conclude that Jesus had let me down. I asked and did not receive. I sought and did not find.

Nor could I make any sense of the central Christian theodrama in which a loving God supposedly staged a bloody sacrifice of his only begotten son in order to satisfy his internal sense for justice. The passion play in which the lamb of God was sacrificed to take away the sins of the world revealed a god at odds with himself, a god in need of psychotherapy.

The transcendent God of my childhood religion left me stranded on a double paradox: the more obsessively I struggled for faith, the more my doubts grew. Yet, I was unable to cease searching for a God who was not to be found.

Fortunately, all the while I was anxiously striving to gain assurance of my salvation, I was leading a parallel life as a happy heathen. To misquote Dr. Johnson, I tried to be a Christian, but cheerfulness kept breaking through. And as if to encourage me on my journey, the Unknown G— of ever-mysterious ways ordained that my first preadolescent crush would be on a girl whose natural name was Gay Birdsong!

In contrast to the Calvinism that shaped my psyche to be always anxious and striving, an easy grace descended on me whenever I escaped the embrace of my loving family. All I had to do was take a short walk down Wilson Avenue past my grandmother's house, cross Court Street, and duck under the fence that enclosed the endless acres of the Maryville College Woods. Once inside, all thoughts of God and Jesus and all need for salvation vanished, and for hours I was in a natural state of grace.

On my days alone in the woods, I followed an invisible trail with no destination, which led mysteriously from one bird to another. A slight movement under a bush revealed a Brown Thrasher scratching around in the leaves in search of breakfast; a rapid drumming led my ear and then my eye to a Red-headed Woodpecker circling a dead oak tree; a whirl of wings alerted me to a Ruby-throated Hummingbird darting from flower to flower; nasal cawing drew my attention to a colony of crows who seemed to be in constant communication about some clever, if not sinister, plans; a lyric riff led me toward the edge of the woods, to a clearing where a

golden-throated Eastern Meadowlark sat on a post singing a
solo. In this way the wonders continued: from bluebird to
goldfinch to waxwing to sparrow to mockingbird to warbler
to kestrel to nuthatch to towhee to other birds without end. I
passed from sighting to sighting with no sense of time,
urgency, or self-consciousness. I, the observer, disappeared
into the observed.

In the late afternoon, I would frequently pause in my
wanderings, lie on my back near the stream, and watch the
passing thunderheads change from castles to prehistoric animals to facial silhouettes. As I stared at the shifting patterns,
I began to see myself in a new way. The religious anxieties
and painful self-consciousness that usually troubled me were
replaced by a wondering self-awareness. The great primordial
questions played through my mind. Why is there anything
rather than nothing? Where did I come from? What will
happen to me when I die? If there is a God, what should I
do with my life? If there isn't, what would I like to do? Why
am I such a different person—safe, spontaneous, excited,
complete, without doubts or any sense of failure and guilt—
when I am in the woods watching birds? Do other people
wonder about things like this?

It was in my wanderings in the woods that I first experienced a place apart from my parents' world—a place in which
my wildness and native sense of the sacred could emerge.
Within the unfathomable vastness of the Maryville College
Woods (perhaps three hundred acres), the numinous was as

palpable as the fluttering of a thrush in the bushes, as audible as the creek music, as redolent as the acrid perfume of the pines through which the wind sighed. The landscape itself and the creatures that inhabited it were more like presences than material objects, and I was continuously in a mood of hushed reverence.

Within this spiritscape, G— was present, not absent; proximate, not remote; familiar, not strange; manifest, not hidden; the source and ground of my enthusiasm, not a distant, demanding deity. Yet, that divinity had no name and required no special acts of worship beyond open-eyed wonder and reverence for life.

And the Indigo Bunting? The bunting was the first of many slant revelations and incarnate metaphors that spoke to me of the primal sacredness of life. They form the basis of my creed, as expressed by D. H. Lawrence: "There is a sixth sense, the natural religious sense, the sense of wonder."

THE EVERLASTING CARDINAL

IN LOVE ABIDING

AS MY ENTHUSIASM FOR BIRDS DEEPENED, I began to discover a secret community of adult bird-watchers who shared a universal language. One day, ancient Daddy Knapp, who lived across the street and never emerged from his home in anything other than a suit, vest, and tie, shuffled toward me on the sidewalk and volunteered that a Baltimore Oriole was nesting in the tree beside his house. He suggested that I might have the basketlike nest after the fledglings abandoned it. When I was invited to give a lecture on local birds to a women's literary club, my circle of informants grew, and miscellaneous neighbors and kind strangers began to tell me about sightings of rare and ordinary species and bring me orphaned eggs for my collection.

My most ardent ally was Miss Hazel Beach, the art teacher at my school. To my youthful mind, she was an adult, a fully grown woman, although I now calculate she must have been about twenty-three. She was vivacious, shapely, raven-haired, given to easy laughter, and totally dedicated to initiating children into the joy of art. She lived a block away and would come out on long summer evenings and roller-skate with the neighborhood kids under the streetlight on the smooth stretch of Court Street. She was the only adult we kids knew who both played with children and maintained her dignity and authority. Because she was different and lovely, parents who valued propriety above vitality were suspicious of her. Why was a young, attractive, unmarried woman playing with children?

Because I had visions of becoming an illustrator of bird books, I enrolled in Miss Beach's after-school art class. My first project was to draw a cardinal sitting on a bare twig.

In real time, the time in which objectively identifiable events happen, a cardinal is a frequently occurring phenomenon, a superbird that zooms through the air like a flash of lightning and lands on the highest perch in the area. When it starts to sing, out comes an operatic soprano voice. *Birds of America* reports that it is ever cheerful, active, and industrious. The liberated male cares for the young, while the female sits on a second laying of eggs. On gray afternoons in New England, when the only birds that haven't gone south are those scurrying birds—Black-capped Chickadees, White-breasted Nuthatches, Slate-colored Juncos—that specialize in the dark tones of winter, a cardinal will slice through the gloom and land on a branch, bringing a promise of spring potent enough to get you through the dead time.

So much for real time. The cardinal that appears most often to me these days rises from the timeless depth of my memory of the countless weeks that I labored to draw an acceptable Red Bird. The result was always the same: a formal portrait of a cardinal that might be mistaken for an immature Rhode Island Red chicken. In time it became obvious that I lacked the talent to match my passion. In the end, even Miss Beach was forced to admit that the old adage "Anyone can learn to draw" was wrong in my case.

During the course of my failed art lessons, Miss Beach and I discovered our common love of birds and began to develop a clandestine relationship. If we passed in the hall at school, we would share the latest news from the feathered kingdom. Soon, we began meeting after school and on weekends to wander through the College Woods with binoculars and bird books in hand. Gradually, our list of observed and identified species grew. But each time we would spot a cardinal, Miss Beach would laugh and say "Now, that is what a real cardinal looks like." But we both knew that the most real cardinal was the misshapen one that was a token of our shared love.

What was most obvious was her lighthearted manner and the pleasure she took in all living creatures—especially me! While my family encouraged my polite ways and my religious sincerity, Miss Beach delighted in my wildness, mischievousness, rascality, and physical daring. She watched admiringly when I climbed far out on the limbs of a hickory tree to get a glimpse into the nest of a vireo, or grasped the upper branch of a pine tree and rode it to the ground. She listened with mock disapproval, but obvious relish, when I described how I changed all the trail signs made by the Boy Scouts for their pathfinding classes, so that they ended up a mile from their intended destination. Or how my brother and I crept unobserved through the trees and helped ourselves to sandwiches and cake from the overladen baskets brought to the picnic grounds by a flock of women from the church or from the local chapter of the Order of the Eastern Star. Following the telling of such tales, I would often receive a cartoon illustrating the events: bewildered Boy Scouts going around in circles, or stout women wondering what happened to their food. In honor of my exploits, Miss Beach christened me Sambo Kingo the Congo.

On the sad day before I left Maryville, Tennessee, to move to Wilmington, Delaware, Miss Beach asked me to meet her by the old gate on the path that led into the deepest part of the woods. She gave me a scout knife with a wonderful assortment of blades and a promise that we would always be friends.

For several years we wrote to each other. Her letters always contained news of the bird world. "One of my wren gourds has turned out twelve young birds this spring. . . .The cuckoos are making themselves very much at home. Their nest, I discovered, is in the locust tree in the corner of the yard. They are very shy, but sing quite often. . . . I found

the wings of a Brown Thrasher; the family cat had eaten it.
Well, Sam, right after that the cat disappeared, and everyone—that is, almost everyone—is wondering what became of
it. I shall give you one guess as to where the cat went."

Her letters were lavishly illustrated. A cardinal or a goldfinch perched on a bush appeared in the place of a return
address. The head of a warblerlike bird with a blue eye surrounded by a black patch occupied the middle of a page with

a request. "Please tell me what this bird is. I have never seen
a picture of it. This is a memory drawing, so I know it is not
very accurate. Color—something like a Mockingbird with
large spots around the eyes, am not sure but there might have
been a stripe on the head." On one of the rare typewritten
letters, a pale pink flamingo, as faint as a watermark, stands

on one foot. In another letter, one page has been cut and folded so that "a new type of Spoonbill discovered in the imagination of an art teacher" pops out when it is opened. And there is a cartoon of Miss Beach and an art class in

the College Woods, with kids climbing trees, fighting, and chasing butterflies. And off in the corner a frog is saying, "Oh, them again," and a snake is replying, "Yeah."

Sometime in my middle teens I lost track of Miss Beach. Last year I placed an advertisement in the newspaper in Bowling Green, Kentucky—her last known address—and received a letter from a friend of hers telling me Miss Beach had died two years previously. She never married, always befriended children, and kept track of the doings in the bird world.

With Miss Beach, birds were the vocabulary of love that allowed us great intimacy and kept us at a proper distance. Our age difference was too great, and I was too young, for romance. Still, I remember the electric feeling I experienced when I accidentally touched her breast one day as we were skating, and she, ever so gently, removed my hand. Clearly, ours was, in the sense that Plato defined, an erotic relationship. Together we loved beauty, and recognized and honored each other as lovers.

Love, like cardinals that suddenly appear from the wild blue yonder, always seems to be a gift we do not deserve. Love is the opening through which we have the best chance of glimpsing an abiding presence of the sacred within Being itself. In the degree that we are cherished as children or adults, a loving conspiracy is woven around us that undergirds our lives with a sense of the sacred. Love, as Gabriel Marcel, the French philosopher, says, is "a concrete approach to the mystery of being." These days, gathering the memories of the important people in my life, I am reminded that the love freely given to me, no less than my DNA, has informed my trajectory through life, my destiny.

> *Dear Miss Beach,*
>
> *the Cardinal is still crimson*
> *as the blood of life,*
> *and stronger than death.*

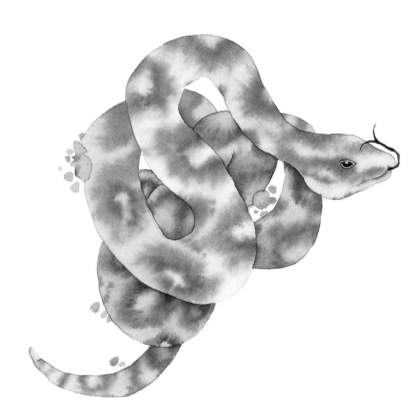

SPARROWS, SAPSUCKERS, AND RATTLESNAKES

THE COMMONWEALTH
OF SENTIENT BEINGS

IN MY YOUNG MIND, SPARROWS FELL into two categories: the uncommon and precious, and the common and expendable.

To the amateur eye, most sparrows are simply Basic Brown Birds. Because they look so much alike—stripped, streaked, spotted, and generally tweedy—they are hard to distinguish from one another. On my expeditions, I would frequently see a small brown blur in a bush, which would disappear before I could study its markings to determine its identity. So I never became a connoisseur of sparrows, although I was often delighted by the lyric singing of White-crowned and Song Sparrows.

English Sparrows were definitely common, uninteresting, and a nuisance. An undifferentiated horde, they invaded farms and inner cities and displaced better birds. They nested en masse in the eaves of ordinary houses, barns, and vine-covered public buildings, filling the air with their continuous chirping and covering sidewalks with their droppings. Store owners along the main street periodically hired a local storm trooper, armed with a shotgun, who went from store to store before business hours to blast colonies of sparrows and pile the bodies on the margins of the sidewalks for the garbageman.

Being a fan of the colorful, the exotic, and the rare, I believed that Scarlet Tanagers, or the interesting sparrows like the Black-throated, the Golden-crowned, or the Lake Sparrow, should be protected, but basic brown ones were expendable. They belonged to the same category of "enemies of higher culture" as starlings—which traveled in gangs like Hell's Angels and were known to augment their daily diet with eggs stolen from other birds' nests—or cowbirds that, in imitation of the jet-setting rich, laid their eggs in other birds' nests, forcing the host to be a surrogate mother. More than once, I had come upon the hanging nest of a diminutive Red-eyed Vireo filled to overflowing with a ravenous baby cowbird, while the ground beneath was littered with the corpses of vireo fledglings who had either starved to death or been pushed from the nest.

As a budding ornithologist, I did not object to the policy of extermination of lesser species. I even furthered it in my own modest way. Like most boys in the pre-television South, I went through the slingshot stage, which came before the era of the BB gun and the twenty-two, and felt it was my right and duty to practice my marksmanship on small moving things. A forked stick, two strips from an old inner tube, a bit of leather, and a few smooth pebbles were all I needed for big-game hunting. After a lot of practice, I was a good enough shot to bag sparrows and starlings and to terrorize chickens and strange dogs that wandered into our yard.

One day in the front yard, while working on my marksmanship to avoid mowing the lawn, an anonymous bird flashed through the sky over my head. Without aiming, I let loose a missile in its general direction, and, to my surprise, it fell dead at my feet. I was horrified to realize it was a Yellowbellied Sapsucker, an exotic bird I had never seen before. I picked up the lifeless bundle, caressed its yellow-gold breast with my finger, and felt deep shame for killing something so rare and beautiful.

After that, I was never able to kill for sport. Although I had no love for the colonies of English Sparrows, I came to respect the bare fact of their livingness. I understood that the great commandment to do justice, love mercy, and walk humbly with God must be translated into the discipline of practicing reverence for all life. I was forced to recognize that all members of the commonwealth, all species rare or common, shared an unconditional will to live, which is the divine spirit within us. Standing, or kneeling, in the presence of the mystery of death and the miracle of life I had carelessly extinguished, I felt that ultimately there was no distinction among sparrows, sapsuckers, and me. I owed reverence, respect, and restraint to all.

Holy happenings don't always involve lovely birds, beautiful sunsets, or lions lying down with lambs, however. They may happen in an encounter with a creature from the dark side of the force.

This spring I came upon the most awesome rattlesnake I had ever seen: a full four feet long, thick as my wrist, and dark green at the head, tapering to lime green by midlength. Only the last twelve inches before the rattles had the dark crisscross lines against a tan background that are typical of rattlesnakes.

Feeling both fear and fascination, I sat down at a safe distance and settled in to observe. Our eyes engaged. Nobody moved. As we remained in our silent encounter, my fear was gradually replaced by a sense of comfortable familiarity. For an eternal moment, I lost my habitual anthropocentric prejudice and found myself empathetically united with the rattlesnake. I was no longer a superior being, but instead a member of a family of sentient beings, all of whom love their way of life no less than I love mine.

As I write this, I can almost hear the sneers and criticism. As though one could have a revelation by viper! What a ridiculous, romantic notion! Modern, normal people don't see symbols in snakes!

In defense of the viper, I suggest that the goddess religions and the healing cult of Asclepius, both far older than Christianity, were wise to recognize the serpent as a messenger between the divinities of the underworld and the heavenly gods. Who better than a creature that yearly sheds its skin to teach us the gospel of the universal cycle of birth, death, and renewal? We are accustomed to the old metaphor of heavenly angels with feathered wings bringing us divine messages, but our age requires dark angels to remind us of the wisdom of the earth. Just the fact that I am amazed to see a wild snake in this paved and manicured world is a vivid reminder of how far we are from realizing that we are all a part of a single ecosystem. In our time, acid rain and deforestation are symptoms of the disease of human hubris that will be punished by plague, famine, and the extinction of many species unless we change our ways. Count on it.

My rattlesnake was such a chthonic angel, an awesome creature who reminded me that we thrive or perish as members of a single sacred commonwealth. Is it foolish to hear in the voice of the serpent an echo of a wandering prophet who taught us that we all are citizens of the Kingdom of God? The task of authentic religion is not to create a biography of G—, but to remind us to tread reverently on the humus and to show compassion to all sentient beings. Any entity, person, or event may become sacramental, whether a dead sapsucker, a living rattlesnake, or the prophets of old.

> *It is the moon*
> *not the finger*
> *pointing at the moon*
> *that calls us*
> *back to ourselves.*

THE WOOD THRUSH

AN ENCHANTING ECHO

IF YOU ARE VIGILANT, you may see a Wood Thrush in the woods of Tennessee at almost any time of day. You can identify the species by its elegant dress. Think of a well-turned-out English gentleman of the old school. The bird's crown is tawny, passing into cinnamon brown on its back and shoulders, giving way to an olive-gray tail. It wears a contrasting polka-dot vest the color of clotted cream sprinkled liberally with blueberries.

At high noon, the thrush hops around in low bushes and seems to have only modest ambitions and domestic concerns—as different from a brash Blue Jay as you can imagine. It quietly goes about feeding on a balanced diet of protein—ants, beetles, grasshoppers, caterpillars—and fruits—frost grapes, blackberries, and wild cherries.

Often, as I would be gathering multicolored rocks with indecipherable hieroglyphic markings from the creek, or searching for a pine tree with chewable amber pitch oozing from its multilayered bark, I would look up to get my bearings and be startled to see a thrush sitting on a nest just above eye level. I could see that thrushes were accomplished architects and builders. They chose a site where the nest would be well supported in the crotch of a sapling, the same spot I would have built a tree house. The foundation of the nest was constructed by inserting twigs, grass, and leaves into a matrix of wet mud, which dried to form a strong superstructure. The plush decor was made of soft grasses and bits of moss. Sometimes, the finished dwelling would be decorated with pieces of ribbon or paper scavenged from the detritus left by humankind. Altogether, the nest offered both domestic security and creature comfort.

Whenever I came on a nest, I knew the rule: look but don't touch. Yet it was my duty as a budding ornithologist to make a careful examination of the state of affairs. If I found that a cowbird had deposited her eggs, forcing the thrush to become a nanny at the expense of her own young, I might remove the offending white-spotted eggs, leaving only the smaller greenish blue ones.

It wasn't until twilight that the thrush changed from domestic diva to shaman. From somewhere far away, a single note from its throat, like a bell calling me to matins, stopped me in my tracks. Suddenly, I was dumbstruck and forgot that I was supposed to be hurrying to the opening in the fence, leaving the woods, and crossing Court Street in order to get home in time for dinner. I stood riveted to the spot, my ears straining to follow the enchanting sound until it disappeared into silence.

The song of the Wood Thrush, or Bell Bird as it is sometimes known, is so haunting that bird lovers have gone to extremes to describe it. In *Birds of America*, it is variously expressed as sounding like "the opening of Weber's Invitation to the Dance; the sweetly solemn thought of Handel's Largo; Faust's beautiful appeal to Margaret in the garden." But not many birders have tried to understand the particular nature of the haunting.

The thrush's song belongs to a family of experiences that usher us into a threshold where sound trails off into silence, time disappears into timelessness, and the known world is engulfed by the great mystery. The family includes the reverberating echo of a temple bell that dwindles off into the void; the polyphonic chanting of Tibetan monks that merges into an endless communal chorus; the electric interval between the crash of thunder and the flash of lightning; the awful emptiness when the exhalation of a dying person is not followed by an inspiration; the deep sigh and profound calm that comes in meditation when the mind finally stops chattering; the timeless moment, before sleep or after awakening, when we enter a dream world in which it seems perfectly reasonable that we should fly, change gender, or simultaneously be ourselves and our parents.

In these threshold moments, the spirit slips between the synapses of the mind. The normal illusion that there is nothing beyond the tyrannical march of profane time (*chronos*) is dispelled, and we have a brief intimation of eternity, an awareness of sacred time (*kairos*). In these pregnant voids we come to understand the limit of our comprehension. We gain a tacit knowledge that our modes of experiencing

time and the world are nothing more than the mechanisms, categories, and paradigms created by our limited minds. Like monarch butterflies confined on their migrations to low altitudes, our wings will not carry us into the vast regions of outer space.

The proper name for this experience of unknowing is not mysticism but wisdom. When Socrates was told that the Oracle of Delphi said he was the wisest man in Greece, he replied that it could only mean he knew what he did not know. Wisdom arises from the certain knowledge of our ignorance, and it teaches us that we dwell within a small circle of light surrounded by an immense mystery. According to tradition, the owl—the symbol of Athena, the goddess of wisdom—spreads its wings only with the arrival of dusk. Wisdom is the paradoxical art of seeing in the dark.

There are no Wood Thrushes in the sparsely wooded area of California where I live now. But there are Great Horned Owls aplenty, and when they begin their low, uncanny hooting just after dusk, I am transported back to an earlier time when I stood quietly at the threshold, listening to the thrush's invitation to evensong, and heard a faint echo of the silent music of the spheres. Over the years, the thrush's shaman song has gradually transformed me into an enchanted agnostic. Unknowing. Amazed.

THE MO(U)RNING DOVE

AMBIGUITY AND SOUL

FIRST SEEN OCT. 21, 1941. Twelve inches long, grayish blue above, reddish fawn below, tail longer than its wing, often mistaken for the extinct passenger pigeon. "Its best known characteristic is its call—it can hardly be called a song—which suggests hopeless sorrow, or tenderest love and devotion, according to the mood of the listener" (*Birds of America*).

For some reason, I always have trouble remembering the proper spelling of this bird's name. Is it the Morning Dove or the Mourning Dove? Does it herald the beginning of the day or the end of our days, the dawn or dusk of our trajectory?

I could go to a dictionary or bird book and clarify this matter, but, for now, I will not. Freud taught me that what I forget is significant, and where I cannot resolve an ambiguity, I should look for paradoxes. An ambiguity may point to an unrecognized trove of connected meanings, a coincidence of the opposites. A slip of the tongue may reveal a voice that has not been allowed to speak. Something well known that cannot be recalled may, like a scar, protect an unconscious wound. Where we stumble and fall we are likely to find the treasure. So, for the moment, I will follow the dove into the thicket of memory and ambiguity and see where it leads.

On summer mornings when I was a child, I would awaken on my grandmother's sleeping porch and lie for a long time listening to the joyous cacophony of the various birds that were feeding in the nearby grapevine and tuning up their instruments for a symphony that was never played. The soft cooing of the Morning Dove was like a whisper reverberating in a cathedral. I couldn't tell whether it came from nearby or far away. Like the flickering images of desires that have not yet become clear to the conscious mind, the echoing song seemed to call me forward into the future. Huddled under the blanket, I would imagine the kaleidoscope of possibilities that lay before me that day. I might get my brother, Lawrence, to help me build a dam on the creek near the picnic grounds. I might go to the post office with my grandmother and earn twenty-five cents for carrying the packages she was mailing. I might explore deep into the woods, where dangers may lurk. I might make rubber guns and provoke a battle in the ongoing war with the Long brothers. I might take fifteen cents and the top from a Wheaties box to the store and redeem them for a flashlight to explore the crawl space beneath the house. I might work on my tree house. I might . . .

When I was young and bushy-tailed, the Morning Dove awakened me to the intoxicating notion that my imagination was the only limit to what I might become. All I had to do was choose from the menu of my desires, put on my Levis and Keds, and set forth, and the world would make way for me.

These days it is in late afternoon or dusk that I hear the dove whose name, I have now determined, has to do with mourning. It no longer sings the siren song of the endless possibilities of childhood, but instead the vespers hymn that signals the approaching twilight.

Recently, I went to Ann Arbor to care for my ninety-six-year-old mother, so my sister, with whom she lives, could take a break. Mother is frail but alert. She can scarcely see, hears only with the assistance of powerful hearing aids, must be escorted to the bathroom, and needs help dressing for her only outing of the week, the pilgrimage to the Baptist church. When she needs to go somewhere, I take her arm—fragile as the leg of a foundling that has fallen from its nest, transparent with veins and arteries—and guide her trembling movements through the dark maze she now inhabits. Most of the time she sits quietly and listens to books on tape, or prays for an unknown number of family members, missionaries, and those in peril in the far corners of the earth. I am sure she prays that I will find my way back to the true faith, to the Old, Old Story, but I no longer discuss theological matters with her. Our only prayer together is grace before meals, which she ends with "in Jesus's name," and I end with "bless this food to the nourishment of our bodies."

Tired from a long night punctuated by accompanying Mother on her many trips to the bathroom, I lie down in the late afternoon and fall into a fathomless sleep. Each time I try to struggle to the surface, I am pulled deeper into a vortex of darkness. In this subliminal state I listen to a conversation between two doves. I cannot make out the messages they are sending to each other, or even pinpoint their location. But as their keening continues, it begins to echo through the underground chambers of my being.

The Mourning Dove's song is a ticket to travel, a time machine, a magic carpet that whisks me into the elsewhere. Time past, time present, and time future swirl into a single continuum. The remembered joy of the limitless mornings of childhood alternates with the sadness of the approaching twilight that, before long, will engulf Mother—and me. In my mind's eye, I reverse the direction of time and watch Mother's frail body become young again—a dynamo energizing the activities of the family. She was shy, private, and fiercely Christian even then, but she would occasionally amaze us with stories of the wild flapper years when she would sneak out of her Presbyterian household to dance the Charleston at some Tennessee roadhouse. Or, more often, she would tell how Dad sent roses every Friday to her dormitory at Salem College when they were courting, an extravagant gesture of which she was proud. As the floodgate of memory opens, I am swept along by feelings of both the poignant beauty and the tragedy of time passing. My normal buoyancy and Promethean rebellion against anything that threatens to curtail my freedom—age, disease, death—give way to mourning.

We are grass of the field. We flourish for a season and then fade. Death wipes us out. Yet, we are part of a totality that death cannot eradicate. I was, am, and will forever be a particle within a resurrecting cosmos. My DNA was included in the Big Bang. The blossoming of time, space, and multiplicity intended me, and I will be a part of the unfolding, flowering, and closing of time. I exist within the alpha and the omega.

I admit that I don't know and cannot even imagine what all of this means. But I am convinced that this quantum view of the self is both a demonstrable scientific fact and very nearly what religious people mean when they speak of "soul." To have a soul is to be both a particle and a wave, an individual and part of the whole of being. In one sense, I inhabit only the here and now, the fleeting moment that just passed. Yet, I straddle all the modes of time, living in awareness, memory, and hope. Like the psalmist confronting the complexity of his existence in Psalm 139, I am forced to conclude that the mystery of my self "is too wonderful for me; it is high; I cannot attain it."

Awakening, I hear
two Mourning Doves
calling to each other
over an unknown distance.
Two short owl-like calls, hoo hoo,
followed by three evenly spaced notes.
A haunting duet.
No birdsong is so plaintive,
the whistle of a distant train,
a passing glimpse
through a lit window
seen on a long journey
on a rainy night.
So near, so far.
Like my soul.
Here.
Elsewhere.
Mourning.
Rejoicing.
Longing.

TURKEY VULTURES

SHORTLY BEFORE MY SEVENTIETH BIRTHDAY, I was walking with a friend on a windswept stretch along Lake Michigan. Facing into the wind, sand stinging our eyes, we could scarcely see where we were going. As we came to a section of the beach where the dunes sheltered us from the wind, we noticed two Turkey Vultures circling at low altitude. As we got closer, we saw a magnificent Franklin's Gull, proud in its defiant stance, but dragging a badly damaged wing. As the wing was nearly severed from its body, there was nothing we could do to help, so we were reduced to being spectators of a drama that all but announced itself as "Life Against Death."

An hour later we returned and found the drama had progressed to Act II. The vultures had landed and stationed themselves a short distance from the gull, and were waiting patiently. Occasionally, the gull would raise its good wing and make a painful lunge in their direction to keep them at a distance. Otherwise, he stood his ground—also waiting.

We returned the next day to find out that Act III had been played out in our absence, and the curtain had fallen. The picked-over corpse of the gull was strewn around the sand, the sun bleaching the bones and the wind spreading the feathers far and wide.

Vultures seem destined to be experienced as sinister harbingers of decay and death. My old, romantic edition of *Birds of America* generally has something lyrical to report about most birds, but it can spare no kind words for the lowly Turkey Vulture. "The Turkey Vulture is ugly to the last degree, except in flight, but it is an invaluable health-protector in warm latitudes, where it exists on all forms of carrion, being guided to its food by a sense of sight—not smell."

Ugly, yes, but vultures are marvelously designed for the task of keeping the countryside clean of rotting animals. Their bald heads can be thrust into a carcass without leaving a mess on their feathers. Any remaining bacteria either die on their faces or are killed by the urine they release on their legs. If threatened, the foul vulture employs a form of chemical warfare, hurling the ingested remains of a carcass at an attacker. With the rise in fast cars and superhighways, vultures have become specialists in the growth industry of cleaning up roadkill, and their numbers have increased by 10 percent.

Yet, nobody loves a vulture. Nobody puts up vulture feeding stations, or has pictures of the gangly fledglings on their refrigerators. Like garbagemen, they perform a necessary function but are not revered. They are low-class birds, a sort of flying Mafia that controls a far-flung waste-management empire.

The reasons for shunning these disposal experts are not difficult to discern. Sanitary-waste stations are unpleasant realities that should be kept out of view. "Not in my back-yard," we all say. In this most consumptive of societies, we do not want to be reminded that landfills claim our obsolete products, our industrial corpses, almost as fast as they are created—rendering them out of sight and thus out of mind. But the monster lurks. Detritus, debris, rubble, junk, and all manner of environmental pollutants threaten to overwhelm us even as we are obsessed with personal cleanliness and odor-free armpits.

And there is death. We resist acknowledging that the dark angel will have dominion over us no matter how many vitamins we consume, how much cosmetic surgery we undergo, or how frequently we exercise. The grim reaper is not fooled by Botox. Our culture has made a virtue out of the ancient vice of denying death. No wonder we turn our eyes away from the buzzards that, waiting patiently for the inevi-table, circle the skies above us.

Not all peoples have been so inhospitable to vultures or so phobic about death. Archaeologists excavating the ancient Anatolian city of Catal Huyuk (dating from around 6500 BCE) discovered a shrine in which a vulture appears to be a god or goddess responsible for removing the head and thus liberating the soul of the dead. Murals make it clear that the inhabitants of the city lived in an intimate relationship with their dead. The bodies were laid in open funeral houses, where the tearing beaks of Griffin Vultures stripped the skeletons of soft tissue, in a ritual similar to the Tibetan sky burial. They were then buried within the walls of the houses, placed just under the sleeping platforms, where they remained as bedfellows of the living. The intimate conjunction of life and death is further represented in a nearby shrine, in a dramatic image in which the beak of a vulture forms the nipple of a woman's breast. Mother Nature is a giver and destroyer of life, a carnivorous breast.

Whenever we become aware of the fragility of our existence and the inevitability of death, we stand in the presence of the final mystery and are, at once, terrified and wonderstruck. An authentic experience of the holy is never merely nice, gently comforting, or softly reassuring, because confronting the great unknown source of life and death is bound to fill us with anxiety.

Perhaps that anxiety is misplaced. Remembering that the vultures are always circling, we dare not forget that ten thousand beings are aborning at this instant, and buds are bursting into bloom. When we make a habit of remembering our morality, we gain that bittersweet, tragic sense of life that was so prized by the Greeks. Anxiety invites us to become courageous. Realizing the poignancy of life, we resolve to suck the marrow out of every passing moment.

The death of those we love also has a special way of
initiating us into the terrible beauty of life. On November 4,
1964, knowing my father was gravely ill, I flew from Louis-
ville, Kentucky, to Prescott, Arizona, hoping to arrive before

he died. A friend drove miles along the road to the airport to
intercept me with the news that Dad had died a few hours
earlier. Forty years later, the grief remains sequestered in my
heart. So does the glory. Autumn in Arizona was a riot of

burnished gold aspens dying into winter. I understood, as a son whose father would always be missing, that all beauty and love is fleeting and is given to us in a manner that places an incurable ache at the heart of our mortality. Now, it is autumn in California, and the Osage orange trees are a bouquet of celadon and chartreuse. And once again, I feel the gift of life and the terrible mystery of death.

In the best case, our awareness of mortality and our love for those who have passed over into death spreads out to encompass others and increases our compassion for the whole human family. Within the universal embrace of death, we are all citizens of the same commonwealth. The other is no longer a stranger, the world no longer divided between Us and Them. We are all recipients of a sacred gift and a fearful destiny. Our great obligation is to be reverent toward one another.

I have not yet learned to greet vultures with the enthusiasm I have for high-spirited Black Phoebes, but I do honor them as teachers. Around my farm, they are frequently visible picking through the compost heap in the garden, sunning their outstretched wings on cold days, and holding their silent conventions in dead trees when they have business to conduct. Like the skulls that medieval scholars kept on their desks or that Tibetan Buddhist monks craft into cups, they are icons that remind me to cherish mortality before it slips away. I feel their dark presence circling on motionless wings just beyond the edge of my consciousness. These days they are seldom absent for long. Rationally, I know that in the overall economy of our perpetually changing ecosphere, death is as necessary as birth, and that whatever is not always dying is never living.

Nevertheless, I intend to keep the vultures at bay as long as possible. Dylan Thomas, like the Franklin's Gull, had the right idea:

> *Do not go gentle into that good night,*
> *Old age should burn and rave at close of day;*
> *Rage, rage against the dying of the light.*

THE DAWN CHORUS

SACRED SOUNDSCAPES

In the beginning was Silence.
On the fifth day
God created the birds of the air
and all manner of song.
And God saw that it was good.

Daily, I am entertained by a chorus of birds.

At dawn the crows gather and each caucus loudly
pushes its agenda from a different tree.

A House Wren flits about and scolds like a nagging
housewife.

A Steller's Jay begins a riff with three low-pitched,
raucous blues notes.

A Rufous-sided Towhee kicks and scratches the
leaves under the rosebush and gives an occasional
nasal whee, whee.

*A White-breasted Nuthatch plays a snare drum
rhythm on the side of the oak tree, prospecting
for a tasty bug.*

*A Common Flicker repeats its rapid signature
lick-flick-flick-flick as it flies.
A Red-tailed Hawk gives a series of screams.*

A White-crowned Sparrow trills and whistles.

*Three Great Horned Owls hoo, hoo, hoot to one
another just before nightfall.*

Not long ago, I was surprised to discover that I hear very little. The problem is not with my ears. Although I have lost acuity in distinguishing some consonants in the human voice, I still have the ability to hear the faintest call of a distant coyote on a moonlit night. The fault lies not in my hearing, but in my listening.

Then I met Bernie Krause, a dedicated listener and one-time member of the folk group The Weavers, who changed his profession from playing music to listening to and recording wild soundscapes throughout the world. In his quest for biophonies—creature symphonies, soundscapes of specific habitats or biomes—he has traveled from the Amazon to Zimbabwe, recording everything from jaguars to baboons, from ants singing to the music of the rain forest.

One morning before sunrise, Bernie and I made our way to a remote valley near my home in Sonoma, California, that was well insulated from human noise. Dawn is typically the best time to listen to the birds because there is little wind and sound carries well. Bernie set up his recording equipment, and then we took a seat and waited for the concert to begin.

After a long, cold night and no breakfast, we heard a male bird advertise his virility by the intensity and vigor of his song. Different species of birds and insects roused themselves from sleep at different intervals and began warming up their vocal cords. At first, a few of the featured soloists and supporting vocalists began rehearsing: a host of Song Sparrows practiced the soprano melody; Purple Finches and lesser sparrows added chirps, tweets, and twitters; Mourning Doves crooned the antiphonal moan; ubiquitous crows provided the caws and cackles; and woodpeckers delivered the percussion. As the morning began to warm up, insects beyond number furnished a rich drone composed of hums, buzzes, and the swish of wings. All of this was accompanied by the sighing of the wind and the gurgling of the brook. A few minutes after full dawn arrived, the cacophony seemed to end and the thousand individual creatures began to tune their instruments to a single complex pattern. Gradually, an invisible conductor forged the discord into a unified composition— Symphony in a Meadow on Sugarloaf Mountain—that lasted until the sun was high and hot.

When we turned off the equipment and listened through stereophonic earphones to the recording we had made, I was drawn into a psychedelic soundscape richer than any I had experienced. I was surprised to hear the songs of many birds I neither recognized nor had consciously heard with my naked ears. Additionally, in the distance, I heard the familiar gobble of Wild Turkeys and the soft whirl of hummingbird wings, neither of which I had noticed. But what was most amazing was that the recording revealed not a chaotic collection of random songs and sounds, but a soundscape in which each creature had its unique aural niche. Bernie explained that insects, birds, mammals, and amphibians in healthy habitats occupy sonic niches that allow each creature to express its voice without competition from others. Listening carefully, I could hear the various singers and players respond to one another like members of a New Orleans jazz band.

In subsequent days, as I listened to Bernie's recordings of ants singing, an elk bugling, a jaguar in the Amazon, a lone cricket, and a California forest before and after logging, my ears opened and I began to understand how unsoundly I had been living. Like a new convert who has suddenly realized the folly of his former ways, I felt I had sinned and should recite the old Prayer of Confession, slightly revised: I have neglected the many voices to which I ought to have listened, and have paid attention to chatter, noise, and endless words I ought to have ignored.

When did I abandon the rich soundscape that called to me in childhood, the quack, chirp, whinny, bark, whine, bleat, mew, cackle, hoot, honk, and warble of birds, the whisper or howl of the winds, the splash and swoosh of falling water? When was the last time I fell asleep listening intently to the lullaby of cicadas or the sound of soft rain on a tin roof? And why did I cease listening?

Like most modern people, I am in danger of becoming a prisoner in Plato's cave, a captive in a virtual reality, brainwashed by a barrage of data, e-mails, messages, spam. I am inundated by profane language: I live and move in a mediascape that is constantly hawking merchandise, ideologies, and gospels that promise easy happiness and cheap grace. If I am not careful, my mind and soul will be colonized by the money changers who have invaded the temple of language, destroying the sacred bond between word and truth.

> The noise-to-information ratio grows every day.
> The noise-to-knowledge ratio is unimaginable.
> The noise-to-wisdom ratio is beyond calculation.

In addition, there is the everyday cacophony of automobile horns, airplanes, cell phones ringing, fire engines, ambulances, police sirens, boom boxes, jackhammers, and occasional bombs bursting in air. For anyone who craves yet more noise, the danger of silence can be avoided by the portable music player. The walking wired have eliminated the risk of experiencing a silent moment into which strange thoughts might intrude.

It is difficult to estimate the toll the profane soundscape has taken on us. The omnipresence of noise and speed destroys the rhythm of meditative and contemplative thought. We literally cannot hear ourselves think. We go from word to word to word, instead of from silence to word to silence to word. Our talk is loquacious rather than deliberative. Listening is rapidly becoming a lost art.

When profane words and noise fill every nook or cranny of our time and space, the fertile silence that is an integral part of reverence is destroyed.

It was not always this way. In the beginning, silence was profane and noise was sacred. For most premodern human beings, ordinary life was altogether too quiet. Village life followed the recurring cycle of the seasons. Nothing much interrupted the sounds of rushing streams, waves breaking on the shore, spring rains, wind whistling through the trees, falling snow, the plowing of fields, and the planting of seeds.

On my many visits to Bhutan, I have sat in small villages and listened to the faint sounds of ordinary days: cows chewing, dogs barking, children laughing, prayer flags flapping in the breeze, streamlets burbling, a family chanting *om mani padme hum* as the morning mist lifts—modest sounds barely rising above the immense, encompassing silence of the vast landscape.

Then come the holy days, the great religious celebrations. People arrive from miles around, many traveling by foot or horseback for days to reach the temple compound where the cycle of sacred dances will be performed. On each day of the festival, the hills reverberate with the drone of the great trumpets played by the monks. The narrow valley surrounding the temple is filled with the rhythmic chanting of prayers and the hypnotic beat of drums.

Inside the temple courtyard, elaborately costumed dancers enact epic stories of casting out demons and of founding the Dragon Kingdom of Bhutan, as well as the karmic drama of human life, death, and rebirth. Periodically, raucous laughter breaks out as clowns, using a wooden phallus, simulate sexual intercourse, parody the movements of the dancers, and interrupt the "serious" ceremonies with ribald humor.

Outside the temple walls, a carnival atmosphere prevails. Small booths offer rice, chilies, yak cheese, and roasted meats. Groups of men huddle, playing games of chance with dice. Women sit on the ground, with blankets spread before them covered with weavings, prayer beads, weathered cymbals, bells, and miscellaneous ritual objects. Local liquors flow freely, and greetings and laughter fill the air.

When night falls, the dancers lead a procession down into a meadow. There, hundreds of people gather near a large pine-branch arch for a purification ritual. Lore and tradition promise that anyone who runs through the burning arch will be healed of minor ailments and serious diseases for the coming year. Once the structure is torched, a mass of shouting pilgrims run, push, and tumble their way through the flaming gate to greater health. I made the ritual passage three times and my lingering cold vanished.

The celebrations of Bhutanese Buddhists are more in the mold of Dionysus than Apollo. They are excessive, bawdy, dramatic, and laughter-filled—joyful noise in praise of the Lord Buddha. The day after the festival, the din disappears, the travelers return home, and the village returns to the silent repetition of the ancient round of daily life.

What is the sound of the sacred?
Where might we hear it?

The gateway to the sacred is hidden
in surprising places.

Sitting quietly
I am visited
by radiant beings.

Goldfinch.
Sunflower.
Love at first sight.

Three blue birds
on a wire.
Do, Re, Mi.

Today the wind
whispered to me.
Where have I
been so long?

BIRD BRAINS

THE COSMIC MINDSCAPE

THIS MORNING I AWOKE AT FIVE and couldn't get back to sleep. I had been away for three weeks and the bird feeder outside my bedroom window was empty. I got up, filled it, and thought my regular clients would return in a couple of days. Fifteen minutes later, the first Steller's Jay arrived in a fanfare of trumpets. After another ten minutes, the usual suspects began to arrive: Plain Titmice, Acorn Woodpeckers, Purple Finches, and Chestnut-backed Chickadees.

I lay in bed for a long time pondering the mystery of bird talk and avian intelligence. Jays are bullies, so it is safe to assume that they did not intend to share the good news. Hence, the jays, like Navajo code talkers, were broadcasting in jay talk intelligible only to their own kind. This would suggest that any other species that arrived must know not only their own languages, but also a smattering of a universal language, a kind of avian Esperanto, that gives them minimal access to the communications of other species.

It has always seemed to me that birds were highly intelligent beings that inhabited a parallel reality humans were too unimaginative to understand. The Golden Plover is a good example. A single fact about this long-legged beauty—variously called Brass-back, Greenhead, Pale-breast, Hawk's-eye, and Prairie Pigeon—has formed a kind of ornithological koan in my mind. Plovers breed along the Arctic coast, and once their young are raised, they begin a migration that takes them down the coast of Nova Scotia and over the open Atlantic to the tip of Argentina, a distance of ten thousand miles. How do they do it? What kind of minds do they have? To say they do it by instinct is to paper over ignorance. Nor does that other favorite mode of explanation, an evolutionary process of trial and error, satisfy me.

A number of ornithologists say birds have a kind of primitive Global Positioning System that matches the contours of the earth with a sort of map in their brains, an avian equivalent of Internet driving directions. Some birds are said to observe the sun and stars and practice celestial navigation, or chart their progress by mountain peaks and the wandering course of rivers and shorelines. Maybe, maybe not.

At a minimum, the plovers' heroic journey makes you wonder. Do they have favorite stops along the way? Do old friends look forward to a rendezvous by a tasty little pond? Do they race, giving prizes for each stage of the journey to the bird that completes it first, like the Tour de France? Do they tell stories about previous journeys, or about the year winter was so warm they decided to stay north?

The common assumption that birds are mindless stim-
ulus-response units that sing for sex and survive by blind
instinct has been proven wrong by ornithologists, who have
shown that our feathered fellows are able to plan, learn, and
teach their skills to other birds. Findings from a variety of
recent studies support this claim of complexity. For example,

the vocabularies of song languages are vast and intricate.
Nightingales may sing any one of three hundred songs in their
pursuit of love, and the all-time champion, the Brown
Thrasher, has a repertoire of nearly three thousand. Anyone
who has ever tried to sleep on a sultry full-moon night in the
deep South can testify that a mockingbird will plagiarize an

entire songbook. Parrots carry this skill a step further by learning words and using them to communicate with humans.

Crows, who are reckoned to be among the most intelligent birds, can both plan and invent. Common crows turn twigs into tools to extract grubs from cracks too small for their beaks, and they can pass this skill on to other members of their species. In Japan, Carrion Crows perch by a busy intersection, wait for a red light, and then place walnuts on the road. When the light turns green, autos crush the nuts, and when the light turns red again, the crows gather their bounty.

Thomas Bugnyar, a behavioral biologist, trained ravens to find bits of cheese hidden in film canisters and then to pry open the lids to get the food. Hugin, an especially savvy raven, excelled at this, but Munin, the dominant bird, would rush over and steal the cheese. Hugin, a believer in the superiority of cunning over aggression, changed his strategy. He would pry open an empty canister and pretend to eat the cheese. When Munin muscled in, Hugin would retreat to the canister in which the cheese was secreted while the duped bully searched in vain. From this drama, it is easy to deduce that Hugin's practice of the art of deception depended on mind reading. He had to know that he knew something Munin did not, and to plan to use this knowledge to his advantage.

So, if birds have no neocortex, which presumes that they are capable of nothing more than instinctual, primitive responses, how is it that they are so intelligent? According to

Dr. Erich D. Jarvis of Duke University, birds have neurological clusters that are functionally equivalent to the mammalian neocortex, and these allow them to learn and predict complex phenomena. The vast bulk of a bird's brain is not "primitive" at all, but is instead a robust pallium, or higher-processing center. Bird's brains are different in their organization, but they are not necessarily simpler than mammalian brains. Difference does not mean inferiority. Evolution has created more than one way to generate complex behavior: the mammal way and the bird way.

We human beings seem to have developed a mental-spiritual quirk that tempts us to deny the existence of other types of intelligence. We live in a world that is an inter-connected network of entities—waves and particles—constituting a single universe. Yet, we attribute intelligence only to our own kind. All others are aliens, not members of our tribe. What lies behind this extreme reluctance to experience ourselves as part of a community of diverse intelligence?

The modern mind suffers from a hidden disease, an unspoken nihilism, a secret suspicion that we are ultimately alone in an accidental universe, and that the natural world is nothing more than a complex mechanism, without an intrinsic purpose, that emerged by happenstance. Intelligence evolved from a primal chemical soup of mindless molecules and single-celled organisms that reproduced and died for millennia beyond number before the long march toward complex life culminated in—sound the trumpet!—the human brain. Although chimps use sign language, dolphins click telegraph messages to one another, elephants never forget, and wolves appoint godfathers to look after their young, we persist in believing that we are surrounded by dumb creatures that caw, cackle, howl, and hoot, but do not think or have emotions. We live in a lonely world.

It seems to me that something that deserves the name "intelligence" or "mind" is homogenized into every atom that joins another atom to become a molecule, and in every salmon that returns to its place of origin to spawn and continue the journey of life. It is not unreasonable to find evidence for sacred intelligence in the intentionality that is incarnate in every moment of the cosmic panorama.

As I understand it (which I don't), there was no before or after prior to the Big Bang (excuse the paradoxical language). Nor was there a here or there. Time and space happened inside the bang (if we can speak of an inside where there is no outside). I don't know a lot about astronomy or math and I can't imagine the unimaginable, so all of this is difficult to talk about. But for the fun of it, let's speculate.

(Take a deep breath.) Since the Big Bang quickly blossomed, like a skyrocket on the Fourth of July, into this kaleidoscopic world that contains Indigo Buntings, rattlesnakes, and physicists, and since the eventuality of anything depends on everything else (in other words, if there is no carbon from the stars, there is no human brain, and so on), doesn't it seem reasonable to assume that something like a cosmic form of DNA informed the movement from bang to blossom, during which the ultimate singularity became plural?

This cosmic DNA could be understood as an immanent intelligence, an intentionality, a drive toward becoming that is sequestered in the heart of every particle and being. Perhaps this informing power, what the Greeks called the *logos*, is not exactly what religious people mean by God—an omnipotent, omniscient, transcendent creator of all—but is instead a being in the process of becoming, an ultimate creative power informing an evolving universe.

It is easy to get lost in speculative clouds when the best scientific roadmap of the cosmos we have reads: "You are now leaving spaceless space and timeless time and are coming into the realm of endless space and infinite time in the single universe." This isn't a lot of help when it comes to dealing with the dilemmas of everyday life.

As an individual existing within the limited perspective of my single lifetime, I find it impossible to ascend to some scientific or religious observatory beyond time and space to determine whether chance or God has ultimate dominion, whether the marvel of the plover's migration is due to the fickle finger of trial and error or a designing deity. I need some indication nearer to hand by which I might judge whether or not I exist in a world that has been informed by intelligence.

So, I return to the riddle from which I began: the bird feeder. The avian community has gathered and all its members are jabbering at once. They are tuned in to one another sufficiently to know when it is their turn to get in line for the sunflower seeds, but no one is really listening. The Rufous-sided Towhee is happily chirping and biding his time beneath the feeder, waiting for the spilled seeds. The jays are having a raucous conversation and getting ready to crash the line. Three gray squirrels are calculating the daring leaps and alpine maneuvers necessary to make a frontal assault on the feeder. It is a noisy but orderly breakfast.

As I ponder the complex chatter, song, and dance, I feel my membership in the community of sentient beings. And this brings me a sense of comfort and release from loneliness. It undercuts my human chauvinism, the arrogant assumption that I belong to the only species endowed with reason and rights.

Many pre-technological peoples had myths of paradise lost and paradise regained. The stories went something like this: Once upon a time, humans and animals understood each other's language. But humans fell from grace into alienation and began to speak in a babel of languages, which meant that they could understand neither one another nor the animals. Only a few shamans retained the ability to communicate with other species. Someday, the myths promise, the golden age will come again when lions will lie down with lambs and we, like Saint Francis, will be able to talk with the birds, or, like Padmasambhava, ride on the backs of tigers. In that time of second innocence, each species and people will keep its particular tongue. But those who speak Hebrew, Arabic,

English, French, and so on will understand the language of tiger, owl, fox, or daffodil, and vice versa.

This morning, outside my window, a heathen Pentecost is in progress. The bird people from the nearby heath have gathered and are speaking in many tongues: avian glossolalia. Although none understands the literal language of the others, a common spirit animates all of them. In the metaphorical, or spiritual, sense, Pentecost is any moment when we awaken from the cacophony caused by our illusions of separateness to the realization that we are all members of the billion-tongued symphony of being.

The mythical time when individual sentient beings will be joined in a kingdom of G— is this very moment, whether or not we choose to be aware of it. If flycatchers lost their eros for flies, if predator and prey ceased to understand each other's ways and means, if oak trees and lungs refused to continue the dialogue between oxygen and carbon dioxide, and so on ad infinitum, the world would fall apart. The kingdom of G— is an infinite number of interlocking conversations, a World Wide Web extending into the boundless past and the endless future and joining a numberless host of entities into a single living universe that is the dwelling place of Each and All.

WILD TURKEYS

DWELLING AMONG FAMILIARS

WHEN I WAS GROWING UP IN TENNESSEE, it was widely agreed by the local hunters that Wild Turkeys were the wiliest birds, difficult to spot and nearly impossible to ambush. They walked through woods and grasslands as cautiously as settlers in a wagon train going through Apache territory, with wary scouts giving advanced warning of lurking danger.

Hunters prepared themselves as if going to war, making use of every advantage science or magic could offer. First came camouflage clothing—pants, shirts, coats, hats, socks, shoes—with a thick patina of artificial leaves and moss to render the huntsman invisible to his prey. Next came a dazzling variety of calls that promised to produce the siren songs necessary to lure the curious or amorous to their doom: old-fashioned wing-bone and box calls; wooden pot-and-peg calls; and gadgets that gobbled to simulate the mating call of the male turkey, yelped in imitation of the social call used by both sexes, and cackled to replicate the sound of hens leaving the roost in early morning. There were calls that reproduced the cluck and purr of a contented flock, and that duplicated the special sound hens make to locate and excite males. Should all these devices fail, the knowledgeable hunter knew to lure romance-hungry males with painted decoys that were equivalent to the Playmate of the Month.

Throughout American history, the Wild Turkey has been held in high esteem. Both the Indians and the early settlers, who evidently had greater wilderness savvy than modern hunters, stalked them successfully and enjoyed their presence as honored guests at the first Thanksgiving. The communal virtues of the Wild Turkey led Benjamin Franklin to suggest that it should be our national bird: "For my own part I wish the Bald Eagle had not been chosen the Representative of our Country. He is a Bird of bad moral Character. He does not get his Living honestly. You may have seen him perched on some dead Tree near the River, where, too lazy to fish for himself, he watches the Labour of the Fishing Hawk; and when that diligent Bird has at length taken a Fish, and is bearing it to his Nest for the Support of his Mate and young Ones, the Bald Eagle pursues him and takes it from him. . . . The Turkey is in Comparison a much more respectable Bird, and withal a true original Native of America. . . . He is . . . a Bird of Courage, and would not hesitate to attack a Grenadier of the British Guards who should presume to invade his Farm Yard with a Red Coat on."

These days, in the wilds of Northern California, you don't require stalking skills, camouflage, or simulated calls to make the intimate acquaintance of a rafter of turkeys, only patience. My introduction to the turkey clan began a few years ago on a warm summer morning when my stroll along the creek was interrupted by a scurry of poults rushing into the brush for protection. They were acting at the behest of a large mother hen that advanced toward me at a stately pace. I retreated until it was clear by her abandonment of the threatened assault that I was at a safe distance, and then I sat quietly in full view. After a while, she beckoned the bevy out of hiding and all continued their morning foray. The next morning, I returned to the feeding ground, sprinkled a gener-ous offering of cracked corn, waited for the flock to appear, and was rewarded to observe them bustling about in obvious pleasure at finding the prepared feast. I continued my seduc-tion for a month, each day sprinkling the corn nearer to the house, until the rafter got in the habit of appearing in my front yard shortly after dawn to let me know, by a gobble-gobble-gobble chorus, that it was breakfast time.

Around the Fourth of July, the hens, chicks, and wan-dering toms claimed the area surrounding my house as their homestead. They took to roosting at night in a tall oak tree by the creek and flying down in awkward squadrons for break-fast. Should I linger in bed, they flew to the top of a garden fence and walked back and forth and stared into my bedroom window. Throughout the day, if they were anywhere near,

I would produce my best gobble and they would answer. Once or twice a day, one of the matriarchs would come up on the porch and watch me through the glass door as I wrote. None ever entered the house, but I had no doubt that it would be invaded if I left the door ajar.

Occasionally, my calico cat, Calypso, in the grip of feline dreams of glory, would go out among the twenty-five or so adolescent turkeys and begin to stalk one of the birds, slinking around slow and low to the ground, oblivious to the fact that she was in plain view of all. Immediately, nine or ten turkeys would nonchalantly form a circle around her and

continue their grazing, at which point Calypso would lie down and stretch in the grass as if to say, "I was just kidding." For the time being, a truce was called.

When breeding season arrived in early spring, a delegation of musky males appeared at the homestead, in fine feather, to begin their courtship. Dandies on parade, they strutted around before an admiring audience of potential brides. Dark tail feathers with buff bands at the tips were spread in full fan. Breasts in iridescent bronze and green were puffed to the maximum, like weight lifters at a bodybuilding contest. Wattles turned bright red in the excitement of courtship. After several days, the mood of the display changed from finery to ritual combat. Pairs of young toms, full of testosterone and hope, honed their combat skills by squaring off and pushing against one another like offensive and defensive linemen or sumo wrestlers. Encouraged by winning preliminary bouts, the brave few challenged the old patriarchs. The friendly pushing and shoving then gave way to an exhausting struggle in which the combatants encircled one another's necks and wrestled in earnest for hours to establish dominance.

To the victors belonged the spoils; to the losers, exile from the band. Fighting time was followed by breeding time. For turkeys, at least, the axiom attributed to General George Patton seems to hold: "Them that does the fighting does the fucking."

To my eye, the mating dance between male and female was nearly nonexistent. The female squatted, hugged the ground, and waited for the male to mount. Slam, bam, thank-you ma'am. With their mission accomplished, both dusted off their feathers and went in opposite directions. Several times a lone hen unaccompanied by any suitors came up to where I was sitting on the wall, humbly assumed the breeding position, and waited. She showed no fear when I stroked her back. After a while, she got up and wandered away.

Over time, my relationship with the turkeys grew more intimate and complex. Whenever I emerged from the house, they appeared to be observing me closely and took to following me around the property. Before long, they began to accompany me on the first quarter-mile of my daily run. They seemed to have something in mind that only became clear when they began to jump up and flog me with their wings. I was being given the fraternity rush, invited to be a member of the clan. The flogging was their way of letting me know that I was being accepted into their community, though I was expected to assume an inferior place in the pecking order. I never did discover the nature of my duties and privileges because I, uncivilly, carried a long stick that I employed to ward off the sharp claws of my erstwhile kin. As I had done in high school, I refused to accept the hazing that accompanied the rite of initiation.

Nevertheless, my acceptance into the bird clan created something of a Copernican revolution in my consciousness. Like most people who love nature, I had a liberal attitude toward birds and other animals (though not mosquitoes!). I was a good patriarch, responsible to protect those creatures beneath me on the great chain of being. It was my duty to provide refuge and make sparing use of animals that must be killed for me to survive. As the turkeys increasingly treated me as an interesting stranger rather than an enemy, I began to feel that I was living among familiars who shared a habitat, that I was a member of a diverse community that included the local deer, bobcats, foxes, coyotes, mountain lions, squirrels, raccoons, skunks, and myriad species of birds. Together we inhabited an indivisible commons in which each of us had a special niche. By what sophistic logic could I deny that the fundamental law of morality—"Love your neighbor as yourself"—should govern all the inhabitants of the small commonwealth at the end of Norrbom Road in Sonoma.

I worry that the underlying philosophy of the modern ecological movement is liberal rather than radical. It still casts birds, fish, and other animals in the role of others who must be protected, and holds to one law for us and another for them, rather than seeing ourselves and them as members of a single family of sentient beings who will either dwell together or die together. To consider animals as familiars and coinhabitants is alien to the sensibilities of urban dwellers. Should we insist on the principle of the radical communion of all living beings, we would be troubled by a host of questions for which there are no easy answers. For instance, if we respect the rights of other species, are we morally obliged to become anti-vivisectionists? Or vegetarians? Are we obliged to protect the habitat of gray wolves and grizzly bears to the extent that we become opponents of urbanization and economic growth?

These are agonizing questions, and will remain so. But for the moment, we need to bracket them as koans that must be solved by present and future generations and focus on the fundamental question we must answer before we can make any headway on an ecological ethic. How shall we live on this fragile earth?

The German philosopher Martin Heidegger made a distinction between "dwelling," or creating a spiritual and physical home, and "inhabiting," or merely occupying a house or apartment as a "machine for living." Increasingly, inhabitants of the global economic order are warehoused in rectangular grids with walls and fences that protect privacy and rights of individual owners of property. Within these artificially separated spaces from which all strangers may be excluded, we are able to retain an illusion of safety and control. Gradually, our knowledge of the world shrinks and we lose our sensual relationship to our surroundings. In a few short generations, we have moved from dwelling on the land to squatting on its surface, from being at home in fields and forests to being aliens in any wilderness we cannot domesticate, fearful of any animals we cannot control.

I cannot escape the feeling that I am swimming against the stream of modernity. Like my turkeys, there is something awkward and ancient about me. The old vision of what it means to be human, my legacy from the Christian tradition, is still lodged in my body. The story goes something like this: To be, is to be incarnate. I become embodied by being in place. I discover my being through my relationships. I may dwell on earth in a spirited manner only by creating hearth from landscape, living with others in a community built on respect, curiosity, acceptance, and care. The stories of all those who live in the spiritscape I inhabit are woven into my story, and I know them not as specimens but as presences. They are members of that complex community within which I live and move and have my being.

Winter is coming. The rains began last week. Already the creek has risen a foot above the bridge, marooning me for several hours. My small band of turkeys has disappeared for a time, and even my offerings of corn do not lure them back from their wanderings. I know they are somewhere up in the hills, joining up with other bands. One day soon, they will march across the lower field seventy or eighty strong. The expanded band will include a number of partial albinos and turkeys with strange markings I have not seen before. These strangers will not risk accepting my corn offering. Most likely, I will not see any of my flock until spring. I will miss them, as I do my adult children, but will find solace in the community of chickadees, nuthatches, and migrating wax-wings that grace my feeder.

Fine feathered friends!

THE LORD GOD BIRD

THE G— OF SECOND CHANCES

UNTIL LATELY, NO ONE WAS CERTAIN when the Ivory-billed Woodpecker was last seen. Some claim the most recent verified sighting was in 1940. Others say 1970, or 1983. The *New York Times* states categorically that it was 1944. The exact time of the death of the Lord God Bird—as it was called by those astonished Southerners who saw a twenty-inch bird with a thirty-inch wingspan sweep into view, mount a dead tree, and pound on it like John Henry with a hammer in his hand—is not so important as the certain knowledge that it largely disappeared from sight sixty-odd years ago and had been considered extinct.

In 1942, when I was eleven years old and living in Maryville, I was such an avid student of birds that I had identified most of the common varieties in the area. And I was painfully aware that it was too late for me to see the Lord God. I might encounter minor manifestations of the great mystery—Brown Creepers, American Dippers, and Red-headed Woodpeckers—but I would never reach the apex of the great ornithological chain of being. Like Nietzsche's madman, I arrived at an untimely moment in human history, too late for the arrow of my longing to reach the object of my desire.

Nevertheless, I frequently opened my well-thumbed copy of *Birds of America* and dreamed of seeing this magnificent bird, the largest of all North American woodpeckers: big as a crow and adorned with a bill three inches long that resembled an ivory dagger, a flaming red crest, and black body plumage with a white line, the shape of a Z, that extended from the bill down the sides of the neck to the upper flanks. At rest, its white wing feathers folded over its back like an elegant set of tuxedo tails. Its astonishing strength and vigor were illustrated in a report by Alexander Wilson who, nearly two centuries ago, wounded one and confined it to his hotel room. "In less than an hour I returned, and on opening the door he set up a distressing shout, which appeared to proceed from grief that he had been discovered in his attempts to escape. He had mounted along the side of the window, nearly as high as the ceiling, a little below which he began to break through. The bed was covered with large pieces of plaster, the lath was exposed for at least fifteen inches square, opened to the weather-boards; so that, in less than another hour he would certainly have succeeded in making his escape." T. Gilbert Pearson, the editor of my 1940 edition of *Birds of America*, reckoned that this bird of deep-forest solitude was nearly extinct, a victim of encroaching civilization. "A few might persist in the almost limitless swamps of Florida, but so far as the vision of the average man is concerned, the bird has already gone the way of the Dodo and the Great Auk."

In the unrestrained innocence of my young imagination, I continued to nurture a tenacious hope for a sighting of this rarest of American birds. One day, a chance meeting at my grandmother's house converted my improbable hope into a distinct possibility. During the Depression, my grandmother Katherine McMurray, a professor of home economics at Maryville College, started The College Maid Shop, where poor girls from the hills could earn their way through college by sewing. Inevitably, some young woman would find her way into the house at 111 Wilson Avenue and stay for a year or two. Thus, I met Vernida.

Vernida was about seventeen years old, a shy girl raised in a mountain hollow so deep that the smoke from the wood stove never reached the crest of the hill. She was raven-haired and might have been beautiful but for a certain awkwardness that came from not being at home in the city. Before long, we grew to be fast friends. She became infected by my enthusiasm for birds and began to accompany me on my daily expeditions into the woods. One fateful day, I showed her the picture of the Ivory-billed Woodpecker and shared my impossible dream with her. Her response was immediate: "We have lots of peckerwoods like that in the swamps near my house."

I was both skeptical and excited. Not wanting to culti-
vate any false expectations, I opined that she probably had
not seen an Ivory-billed Woodpecker, but rather, its common
cousin, the Pileated Woodpecker, who is slightly smaller,
lacks the white tuxedo tails, and has a high-pitched, perfectly
regular call like that of a flicker, but in a lower register. By
contrast, the Ivory-billed's call sounds like one of the bulb
horns once used on rickshaw taxis, like a New Year's Eve
party horn in the hands of a child, or like the honking of
a flock of Canada Geese in flight. In size, call, and volume
of drumming, the Red-headed Woodpecker is a violin, the
flicker a viola, the Pileated a cello, and the Ivory-billed a bass
fiddle. But in spite of pictures and descriptions, Vernida
insisted there were Ivory-billed Woodpeckers aplenty
in the hills and swamps near her home. And to prove her
point, she invited me to come home with her during Easter
vacation.

I happily accepted, but as the time grew near, I got
increasingly nervous. My folks were too tolerant to talk about
hillbillies, but that was the common name given to people
like Vernida who lived in the remote valleys of the Cumber-
land and Smoky mountains. I had never been in homes that
didn't have electricity and indoor plumbing, and the thought
made me uncomfortable. In the end, the possibility that
I might see an Ivory-billed Woodpecker overcame my hesita-
tion, and the week before Easter we took the bus to Pikeville,
Tennessee.

Pikeville, in those days, was the kind of town Walker Evans might have photographed and James Agee might have described as "hard-bitten" and "near to the bone." Incongruously, our bus was met by an expensively dressed woman driving a Lincoln Continental—a Lord God car among the Model A Fords. She turned out to be the angel who had given Vernida a college scholarship. After lunch and conversation at the only café around, she drove us back into the hills. The pavement gave way to gravel and the gravel to clay before we reached Vernida's home, an unpainted farmhouse in a loose cluster containing a large barn, corncrib, hog pen, spring house, enclosed garden, woodshed, and outhouse. Her sunburned, overalls-clad father, Vernon, and mother, Viola, and a gaggle of younger sisters greeted us, followed shortly by a couple of teenage brothers who had been watering the workhorses down at the creek.

It was all strange, fascinating, and, for me, frightening. In the unadorned, poor, but well-scrubbed household, I was awkwardly polite and out of place. I ate the fried chicken, whose bloody, headless last dance I had seen shortly before dinner; the biscuits; and the apple pie; but I couldn't get the newly churned buttermilk past my nose. Bedtime arrived and, having seen no indoor plumbing other than the hand pump beside the kitchen sink, I asked where I could find the bathroom. I don't know who was more embarrassed, Vernida or me, when it was gently pointed out that the only "bathroom" was the outhouse.

Late Friday afternoon, a handful of men from nearby farms arrived with their best foxhounds—trembling with excitement in their cages—in anticipation of the hunt that was to begin between nightfall and moonrise. Unfortunately, the lassitude I had been feeling all day blossomed into a high fever, and Viola put a hand on my forehead and insisted that I stay home. As the men and dogs erupted into a chaotic mob headed for the creek bottom, the starting point for the hunt, I sat on the front porch and fell into a deep well of disappointment. I had lost my one and only chance to go foxhunting.

After they finished with their kitchen work, Vernida and Viola joined me on the porch. Soon, the random barking of the dogs gave way to a unified chorus of a baying pack in hot pursuit of the fox, and the commentary on the hunt began. Vernida and Viola were as skilled in the idiom of the foxhunt as any sports commentator on television. "They raised the scent down by the stand of sycamores, and they are running up the valley toward Baird's place. You can hear Old Bell leading the pack. Her voice is the one with the deep, sad bellow. She is the best hound there is in staying on the scent." A few minutes later the chorus split into antiphonal voices. "Now you can tell the fox doubled back and changed directions. Suzy always gets mixed up when this happens and keeps going on the first track until she has completely lost the scent. But the fox can't fool Old Bell. She turned as quickly as he did and took a few of the hounds with her, and they have followed her all the way over the ridge. That's why their voices seem so far away." Sometime near midnight, after a chase through Byzantine forest corridors, the fox was cornered and the dogs became a yapping mob anticipating a kill. "Do they always kill the fox?" I asked. "Not always," Vernida replied.

I was secretly repulsed by the image of the fox being torn apart by the dogs. The proprietor of the feed store in Maryville kept a beautiful red fox in a cage in the front window. On my walk home after school, I would often detour

past the store to visit the fox. At night, I would imagine a scenario in which I slipped into the store, opened the lock on the cage, and let the fox return to the wild. Later, he would see me in the woods, recognize me as his liberator, and we would become companions. Not wanting to know whether the hunt ended tragically for the fox, I went to bed.

By morning my fever had vanished. I split some kindling for the wood stove and stayed in the background while preparations were underway for the weekly trip into town. I wanted to poke around the farm and look for birds, so I decided to stay home with Vernida's three younger sisters, who were going to pretty themselves up for the box-lunch social at the school that evening. I spent several hours doing my kind of hunting, observing Barn Swallows, Brown Thrashers, meadowlarks, mockingbirds, and several nondescript yellowish warblers that only experts could tell apart. There was nothing exotic to add to my list of sightings.

Nothing exotic, that is, until I went back to the house, opened the door to the living room, and found a trio of naked jaybirds. Vernida's three younger sisters were playing in and around a galvanized tub half filled with water. Immediately, they surrounded me, pushed me down on the couch, and made it clear that I was to help them practice the art of kissing, in case they should need it at the box-lunch supper. Embarrassment descended upon me. I seem to remember that a few fleeting kisses landed on me before I escaped with a warning from Veronica, who was twelve years old with a hint of buds ready to blossom, that I had better bid on her box lunch that evening.

Come evening, we all went to the one-room school, where a country social was in full swing. Square dancing and cakewalks were preludes to the bidding for box lunches, an event as charged with promise and threat as any debutante ball.

A man's friends would frequently conspire to keep upping the bid to the reasonable maximum before yielding. It was expected that husbands would prove their fidelity by bidding whatever was necessary to fulfill their duty and win the pleasure of eating fancy sandwiches with their wives. Among the unmarried set, bidding was a closely watched declaration of romantic interest, and the competition for a popular girl could get heated. It was not uncommon to spot young swains counting their money to see if they could remain in the bidding wars.

To bid or not to bid—that was my dilemma. Both options were terrifying. Vernida had already gone to the highest bidder, so it was up to me to bid for Veronica, who kissed but did not tell. Once the bidding started, her brothers egged me on, and for the extravagant sum of two dollars and seventy-five cents, I won the hand of the maiden. We went to the darkest corner of the room, talked shyly, and ate our egg-salad sandwiches and chocolate cake. No mention was made of kissing.

Sunday was the day I had been looking forward to because we were to ride horses and mules for six miles, through woodland and swamp, to church. Since Ivory-billed Woodpeckers were known to hide in virgin forests and swamps, this was my best chance to spot one. I was favored with the riding horse and the polished plantation saddle, and our journey began. For an hour or more we wended our way along a faint path that passed alternately through heavy woods and watery ground that squished under the horses' feet. My attention was divided between striving to match the rhythm of my rear end to the rhythm of the horse's, scanning the treetops for woodpeckers, and trying to dodge low-hanging branches. I reached the church and happily dismounted with no sightings, a scratch across my cheek, and a tender derriere.

The church was served by an itinerant preacher who, mercifully, was ministering to some other congregation that Sunday. I only had to suffer through a few verses of "The Old Rugged Cross" and "I come to the garden alone when the dew is still on the roses," and endure an endless prayer, before we adjourned to the tables under the trees for a picnic of fried chicken, green beans, corn bread, iced tea, and sweet-potato pie, to name just a few of the elements of communion. Our return trip to the farm passed uninterrupted by any ornithological miracles, but I did sit the saddle more comfortably and let the horse lead the dance.

At breakfast the next morning, Vernida announced that her brothers were going to get a mess of squirrels and would take me to a place where they frequently saw Ivory-billeds. Provisioned with a thick bacon sandwich apiece and two twenty-twos, we set out. It soon became obvious that, while I was still in the slingshot and rubber-gun stage, the brothers had advanced to expert sharpshooters. In short order, they bagged six squirrels, with six shots through the eyes, so as not to ruin any of the meat. Suddenly, one of the brothers said "there's one" and raised his rifle. I saw movement in the tree, but before I could focus, a shot rang out and a wood-pecker fell to the ground.

I was immobilized by ambivalence, caught between horror and fascination, nausea and excitement. I wanted it to be the rare Ivory-billed Woodpecker and I didn't. At last the object of my desire was literally within my grasp, but I was afraid to touch it.

The shooter picked up the limp and mangled body and handed it to me. What happened next remains a blur. I deliberately did not look to see whether the telltale bill and markings, which had been nearly destroyed by a bad shot, belonged to an Ivory-billed or a Pileated Woodpecker. I did not want to know. I couldn't stand the guilt of wondering if I had been an accomplice to the murder of the Lord God. Had my lust to see the revelation of the mystery profaned and destroyed it? I wanted the sacred thing to remain wild and illusive, and I wanted to possess it. I plucked a few feathers at random and put them in my pocket. Then I laid the remains of the bird in a grave I hastily dug in the hillside and covered it with a large stone.

When we got back to the farm, the story was told and I showed my trophy feathers, but I insisted that I couldn't tell from the corpse what kind of woodpecker it had been. For Vernida and her family, it was not important. Silence descended on the matter and it was never spoken of again.

But the issue was not resolved for me. Back in Maryville, I mounted the feathers on a poster board and lettered above them: "From an Ivory-billed Woodpecker, seen near Pikeville,

Tennessee." In truth, I suspected the dead bird was a Pileated Woodpecker, but I could not resist the simultaneously shameful and prideful claim to possess a relic of the Lord God Bird, an outward and visible proof of what I viewed as an earthly divinity. Presumably, I bear no responsibility for the extinction of the Ivory-billed Woodpecker. But I have never been able to shake the disturbing thought that the very intensity of my demand for a personal revelation, a verified sighting of the Lord God Bird—like the demand to see the face of God— could have been responsible for the destruction of what I most desired.

Postscript.

This story was written in the early days of March 2005, some sixty-two years after it happened, and was set aside to simmer and age. On Friday, April 29, 2005, the second coming of the Lord God Bird was announced on the front page of the *New York Times:* "Deep in the Swamp, an 'Extinct' Woodpecker Lives. The ivory-billed woodpecker, a magnificent bird long given up for extinct, has been sighted in the cypress and tupelo swamp of the Cache River National Wildlife Refuge here in Arkansas, scientists announced Thursday. . . ."

Predictably, no sooner had the faithful announced "the bird is back from the grave" than the doubters began to question the resurrection. Three ornithologists (bound by belief in scientific method to deny singular events and miracles) declared that the evidence presented fell short of proof and demanded an absolutely clear photograph and a bird that could be seen repeatedly by a variety of observers.

Meanwhile, the merchants in Brinkley, Arkansas, have remained as unruffled by the quarrels of ornithologists as the bishops of Rome were undisturbed by conflicting accounts of the resurrection of Jesus. The Lord God, dead or alive, brings the promise of economic revival. The Ivory-billed Woodpecker has been renamed "the million-dollar bird," reflecting the belief that whoever gets a photograph of the bird can sell it for one million dollars. Expecting a bonanza of tourists, entrepreneurs are offering woodpecker haircuts, Ivory-billed burgers, and T-shirts emblazoned with the question "Got Pecker?" And they are preparing for the influx of serious researchers, scientists, journalists, and flocks of passionate bird-watchers who, for the unforeseeable future, will need to be outfitted with camouflage clothing, canoes, telescopes, listening devices, and guides to lead them to the place of epiphanies.

I won't be going.

I believe the lordly bird disappeared because it could not survive the relentless dominion of Mammon. It should be left alone. Sacred things are best shrouded by silence and solitude. It is enough for me to know that the G— of second chances still lives in wild places beyond my ken.

SIGHTINGS

THE PASSIONS OF BIRDERS

I AM WALKING AROUND A SMALL LAKE in Glen Ellen, California. As I approach the shore, pairs of Mallards paddle away, staying as close together as high-school sweethearts. A lone swimmer is too far out in the lake to be identified. I focus my binoculars on it and my field of vision is entirely occupied by . . . what? A new bird to me. Immediately, I become single-minded and concentrate on memorizing its appearance. The most memorable feature is the hairdo, a brown, bushy crest that resembles an Afro. Consulting my field guide, I rule out various species of bay ducks and conclude that I am in the presence of a female Hooded Merganser. As I continue to study her, I lose all self-consciousness and become my admiring perception of the other. In receiving the gift of her presence, I feel a strange sense of being honored by an alien but wonderful being, a feeling I have often had on coming upon a bobcat or coyote in the wild. My instinct is to bow down and pay homage, clasp my hands in the ancient gesture of greeting and prayer. *Namaste. Namaste. Namaste.*

I sense that I am not the only one to express gratitude this way. Careful observation has convinced me that birders, far from being just quaint old ladies in sensible shoes and nerdy zoology students, are involved in something strange, archaic, and clandestine—something more like a pagan religion than a hobby, more like Dionysian possession than Apollonian fascination with lists and bird counts on Christmas day. I suspect that the growing numbers of enthusiastic birders are converts to an ancient cult of bird worship that, like the knowledge of herbal medicines, never entirely disappeared from Western counterculture. For all intents and purposes, the decidedly useless, if not wasteful, habit of going hither and yon in search of esoteric varieties of warblers or falcons appears to be a ritual—a fragment of a lost religion. There is definitely something occult, orphic, about the passions of those who go birding, something hidden from normal citizens and orthodox believers.

Historically speaking, it is not the few who adore birds who are eccentric, but rather the many who ignore them. When humans first began to think of themselves as having a spirit that was separable from their bodies, that allowed them to travel in dreams and trance states, birds became the natural symbols of transcendence.

Bird worship is thought to go back to the Old Stone Age and was practiced in various forms by the ancient Babylonians,

Phoenicians, Philistines, Persians, Greeks, and Egyptians. In Egypt, the mythic phoenix (*bennu*) was an emblem of the immortality that awaited those who died, provided they had performed the proper rituals of sacrifice to satisfy the judges of the dead. The phoenix, like the sun and the soul, rose at dawn, burned itself out in the transit of the sky, and died into the darkness, only to be resurrected with the new day.

The worship of animals and birds was so prevalent in biblical times that Moses felt it necessary to warn the Israelites not to corrupt themselves by making a graven image, "the likeness of any beast that is on the earth, the likeness of any winged fowl that flieth in the air" (Deut. 4:17). Saint Paul, in similar fashion, cautioned against those with foolish and darkened hearts who exchanged the glory of the immortal God for images made to look like mortal man, bird, animal, or reptile. There is speculation that prior to 100,000 BCE, a culture devoted exclusively to birds existed in America.

In ancient Greece or Rome, the unexpected appearance of birds, their patterns of flight, cries, and pecking behavior, were signs given to men by the gods. Politicians and generals consulted official augurs to determine if the omens were propitious for waging war, making peace, or holding elections. In private matters concerning marriages and affairs of the heart, every man was a member of the avian priesthood. Each head of household kept a book of private omens and developed his own system of divination.

Nowadays, the practice of augury and the notion of omens have passed out of favor. No one informed by a modern scientific-technological worldview believes that a flock of crows appearing in the Western sky indicates the propitious outcome of a proposed marriage or the winner of the World Cup. Officially, we have put away such magical and superstitious thinking. We believe in cause and effect, the scientific method, and the promise of better things to come courtesy of technology. But beneath the facade of reason, technological intelligence, and faith in progress, the archaic worship of the chronic deities, the gods and goddesses of the earth, is alive and well in the depths of the psyche.

While modern bird-watchers may not actually worship birds, they do resemble a neopagan cult, practitioners of a natural theology. An examination of the spiritual disciplines and rituals of various types of bird enthusiasts, from the most casual to the most fanatic, helps us to understand the phenomenon.

Ornithologists are at the top of the hierarchy, having devoted a lifetime to the study of birds. Most inhabit the hallowed halls of universities and have a flock of graduate students to help them with research and field trips. The range of disciplines necessary for a modern ornithologist would have dazzled Audubon. Sophisticated computer modeling is now used to trace the migratory patterns of different species, while brain scans and other tools of neurophysiology permit the total revision of earlier accounts of the nature of avian intelligence. Garden-variety bird-watchers may stand in awe of the authority of the experts, as Roman Catholics do of the pope and the cardinals, but they are more concerned with appearances of feathered angels than with the theological science of angelology.

Bird-watchers or birders, the least devout of the avian cult, can be compared to plain-vanilla church members who attend Sunday worship but don't get all worked up about religion. They may observe a gaggle of geese or a charm of finches with pleasure, or put up bird feeders by their dining-room windows, but they don't don foul-weather gear and take to the wilds in pursuit of rare species. While they enjoy any bird that appears to them in a normal day, like average laymen of any denomination, they are content with minor revelations and mild pieties.

The rite of passage that marks the transition from novice to communicant is ticking, or keeping a list of birds you have seen. For the fervent, this might include a description of the date, time, place, and circumstance of the first sighting. Tickers come in two varieties, the casual and the fanatic. Some are content with a little black book in which they record the birds they have known and loved. Readers of this book might correctly guess that I belong to this group of tickers. My list is short and contains mostly my neighbors and friends, the common birds with which I cohabit. I share none of the fanatic ticker's passion to accumulate a life list longer than any other ticker's.

In time, many casual tickers are transformed into fanatic tickers, or twitchers, who actively seek out esoteric birds to add to their life lists. Twitchers are given to uncontrollable spasms of excitement when they see a new bird for the first time. Once this enthusiasm strikes, no corner of the earth is beyond the reach of the dedicated pilgrim. They may discover on the Internet that a Peregrine Falcon can be seen in San Francisco's Financial District, a Short-eared Owl in the Okanogan Valley, or a March Antwren near São Paulo, and off they will go in search of the grail, often abandoning family and job. Think of them as the equivalent of Opus Dei, a cult of believers whose happiness depends on a continual quest for a variety of mystical experiences.

Sadly, in any congregation of the faithful there are those who lay claim to experiences they have not had. In the first flush of enthusiasm after encountering a mysterious winged being, as in any spiritual experience, self-deception is a danger. We have such a strong longing for revelation from beyond the boundaries of our normal ego-encapsulated lives, we are in constant peril of creating the experiences we desire. Stringers are birders who brag about gripping rare species, but who are suspected of misidentifying, stretching the truth, or creating what they want to see.

But we have to be careful here. Most visions happen to solitary individuals and are not open to public scrutiny. Obviously, one cannot expect the sighting of rare birds—the Lord God Bird, for instance—to be verified by a scientific

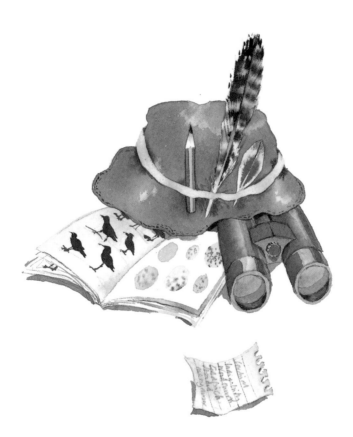

community of neutral observers. Some events that touch the heart and spirit are unique. It is within the range of possibility that a Black-headed Nightingale-Thrush was blown off its migratory course by a tornado and appeared once, briefly, in Bangor, Maine, where it was seen eating its fill of sunflower seeds at Mrs. Hawley's feeder.

Among birders, twitchers are most like the early Celtic monks who practiced austerities on the windswept islands off the coast of Scotland, or Taoist sages who lived by waterfalls in remote Chinese mountains. In their quest for novel religious experiences, they rise before dawn, rain or shine, and proceed to lonely places where they remain in hushed anticipation. Once situated, they quiet their minds by meditation and observe passing thoughts or passing species of winged creatures. Alternatively, they practice single-pointed meditation, holding before their inner eye a devotional symbol—a mandala of Shambhala or an image of a Rufous Hummingbird.

Birders necessarily become specialists in cataloging visions. Faithful tickers develop the virtues of careful observation and ruthless honesty. To confuse a common English Sparrow with a rare Henslow's Sparrow is like mistaking egotism for ecstatic ego transcendence. Obviously, careful observation and discrimination are necessary to determine whether the yellowish bird that quickly flitted across your field of vision was a familiar Magnolia Warbler, or a prized Cape May Warbler to be added to your list.

In gripping a new species of bird—establishing that it may legitimately be added to a life list—appeals to reason, tradition, and authority are necessary. For birders, this involves the discipline of comparing their observation with the sacred scriptures composed by the high priests of orni- thology, the great John James Audubon, Roger Tory Peterson, Arthur A. Allen, David Sibley, and the like.

Although sightings most often occur to solitary individ- uals, bird enthusiasts form a unique community of shared experience. Ultimately, we come to an appreciation of beauty and a sense of reverence for life not through argument or reason, but by association with those who have these sensi- bilities. It takes a community to teach us to see, to feel, and to act in a reverential manner.

In certain respects, birders already inhabit the ideal kingdom promised by both Jesus and Marx, in which there is unselfish sharing of private property for the common good. Each ticker and twitcher contributes to the common- wealth of knowledge according to his or her ability and receives according to his or her need. Should you need a Lewis's Woodpecker to fill out your list of woodpeckers observed, all you do is go to any of a multitude of lists on the Internet and you will find postings by members of the community: Lewis's Woodpecker near Methow, Washing- ton; Tennessee Warbler near Village Green, Los Angeles; Lilac-breasted Roller near Rhino Post Safari Camp, Kruger National Park, South Africa. It is endless. Like the early

followers of Jesus who were said to hold all things in common, birders freely give of their knowledge to one another
and hoard no avian secrets. Theirs is a truly universal community, a form of primitive communism in which membership
is not based on race, religion, or creed.

Birders and other mystics are blessed with a special kind
of vision of the world—the capacity to see eternity in a grain
of sand or the presence of the sacred in the precision flying of
a flock of blackbirds. They are unusually susceptible to the
emotion of awe. When swept away by the appearance of a
previously unseen bird, they enter an altered state of consciousness and experience a momentary state of grace. This
may be seen as nothing more than sentimental nonsense
to the secular mind. But we need to remind ourselves that, to
the color-blind, a description of red is nothing more than an
illusion; to the literal minded, symbol, metaphor, and poetry
are meaningless.

What makes birders of the world unique is their propen-
sity for celebration. In an age in which the major world
religions are marked by serious internal struggles between
fundamentalists and progressives, birders are devoted to a
single-minded pursuit of joyful revelations of what is beautiful and sacred. Their focus is aesthetic, rather than dogmatic
or moral. They belong to the uncomplicated, lighthearted,
religious type that the American philosopher William James
called "the once-born." Life is a gift to be enjoyed is their
guiding maxim. The beauty of winged creatures leads them

from sensual enjoyment to reverence for life. In the wide spectrum of religious types, they are celebrants, practitioners of a theology of nature.

The unexpected appearance of a rare Scissor-tailed Fly-catcher does not bring with it any knowledge about the origin or destiny of the universe or the true name of G—. Instead it reminds us, as the mystic Jacob Boehme said, that we live under a "cloud of unknowing" in a sacred cosmos in

which we may be addressed in extraordinary ways by ordinary events. At any moment an elm tree, a child playing in a sandbox, or the appearance of a mysterious bird may throw us into the most primal of all emotions—ontological wonder—and leave us with the question that can never be answered but must always be asked: Why is there anything rather than nothing?

The secret of life is in plain sight. If we observe with a reverent eye, we may realize that all events, persons, and things are at once ordinary and sacred, factual and sacramental. In a world experienced as sacred, the miracle of the bread and wine is that bread remains bread, and wine remains wine. And an Indigo Bunting may be enough to inspire a never-ending quest for the sacred.